LIVING *through* HISTORY

Th
d

Heinemann

CONTENTS

Britain 1750–1900

Twentieth Century World

BRITAIN 1750–1900, AN INTRODUCTION

Events and ideas

If people living in Britain in 1750 had been transported forward in time, they would hardly have recognised Britain in 1900. Many places which had earlier been just villages or small towns were now bustling cities with what seemed to be huge populations. The ways that people got from place to place had also changed. The way **goods** were made and the way land was farmed were very different. During this period Britain began to change from an agricultural country to one which earned its living through selling manufactured goods. This book looks at some of the major events of the period 1750–1900, and gives you an idea of what it was like to live through some of them.

Trade, the force for change?

The driving force behind many of the changes from 1750 onward was trade. Trade made money. Britain expanded its trading ports, fought to defend them, and acquired an empire. It was important to make cheap goods to trade. Machines were invented and constantly improved to make this possible. Factories were built in towns to make production easier. It was important to move trade goods around quickly and cheaply. Roads were improved, canals dug and railways built at an amazing rate. Much of the money put into these developments came from merchants who would benefit from them.

LONDON BEFORE 1850

Source A

Source B

Even the city of London could seem peaceful and rural in the early 1800s. People in St. James' Park, in the middle of London, could still buy their milk fresh from the cow. The drawing shows St. Martin's Lane in 1825. The church is the church of St Martin's-in-the-Fields.

Industrialisation

One of the most obvious changes that took place was the shift in the way work was done. In 1750 most work was done by small groups of people, using simple equipment. Most people lived in the countryside, and worked on the land. By 1900 a great deal of work was done by machines, many of them in big factories in large towns. Many more people lived in towns, to be close to work. Others were put out of work on the land because of changes in farming.

Things to do

1 Look at the pictures of London in the early 1800s and London in about 1900. The pictures make two pairs.

   a Choose either A and C or B and D and list all the changes that you can find in the pictures.

2 'These pictures are all of London, so they cannot tell you anything about the rest of the country.' Explain why you agree or disagree with this statement.

LONDON IN ABOUT 1900

By 1900 people bought their milk from dairies (shops that sold milk, cream and butter) or carts that went from door to door. Mr Morrison, owner of the dairy and carts in Source C, had the last herd of cows in London, in 1905. Source D shows Trafalgar Square and the church of St Martin's-in-the-Fields in 1902.

Source C

Source D

Leaving the country

Between 1750 and 1900 about fourteen million people **emigrated**. Many went to live in the USA. Most of the rest went to live in British colonies. Some of these were sent there, **transported** as criminals, rather than leaving of their own free will. But others left because their lives in Britain were so miserable that they wanted to make a new life. Many were encouraged to emigrate by landlords who no longer had work for them. Despite this huge drain of people, there were over five times as many people living in Britain in 1900 as there had been in 1750. Why?

More people, living longer

The population of Britain went up sharply for many reasons. By 1900 many towns had better water supplies and sanitation, this kept people healthier. Medical care was better, and vaccines had been discovered to fight disease. People were generally healthier, so lived longer. Babies were less likely to die as soon as they were born (see Source E).

Source E

	1750	1900
Population	7 million	37 million
People living in towns	13%	87%
Life expectancy	Men 31 Women 33	Men 45 Women 48
Deaths at birth	Babies lived / Babies died at birth	Babies died at birth / Babies lived

Britain 1750 and 1900.

Salvation Army midwives visit a mother at home in 1889. A lot of the help for poor families came from organisations like this.

Colonies

As Britain became more powerful it began to acquire colonies abroad, for example in America and India. These colonies helped produce raw materials for British industries and provided places to sell manufactured goods. Not surprisingly, other countries also wanted colonies, and this led to clashes. Britain and France, for example, were great rivals and frequently went to war over control of colonies.

Unrest at home

This was also a time when many working people began to fight for their rights. Britain watched uneasily as other countries in Europe were rocked by discontent among their working people. In France this errupted into a successful revolution and the execution of the French king. British workers, made uneasy by poor living and working conditions and the growing use of machinery to do their jobs, were also restless. They wanted better working and living conditions, the right to form unions, even the right to vote. The government and factory owners were unwilling to change, but they were shaken by outbreaks of violence around the country. They made just enough changes to calm things down.

French and British ships fighting in the Battle of Trafalgar 1805, during the Napoleonic Wars. As a result of these wars Britain gained new land for its empire.

Things to think about

As you read about the various events in the book ask yourself:

- What do the people involved in the event want?
- What actually happened?
- Was this what they wanted?
- Could they have predicted what would happen?

In 1750 Britain was a major trading nation. Its goods were traded across the world by companies such as the East India Company and the Hudson's Bay Company. But at this time Britain did not actually own large areas of land abroad (with the exception of America, which was to win its independence from Britain in 1783).

By 1900 things had changed. Britain had a huge empire which covered a quarter of the world's land mass. Queen Victoria was recognised as ruler by people as far afield as Canada, Trinidad and Australia. How did this happen?

Reasons for the growth of the Empire

During the eighteenth century most British politicians thought that having an empire was not a good idea. Running colonies abroad would be very expensive, and they would require a large, expensive fleet to protect them. Also, politicians feared that having an empire might lead to war.

But in the second half of the nineteenth century these attitudes began to change as the benefits of controlling land overseas became more apparent.

The trading posts which British merchants controlled in 1750 provided good opportunities to sell British goods abroad and to buy raw materials, such as cotton and tea. If Britain owned more places, it would be easier to export goods there and raw materials could be bought more cheaply.

The spread of beliefs

There were many Britons who believed that their country had a duty to spread its beliefs throughout the world. Britain was the world's most powerful country and the people of Africa, Asia and other areas would benefit from being under British control. Then they could learn about Christianity, and modern developments in science, technology and medicine.

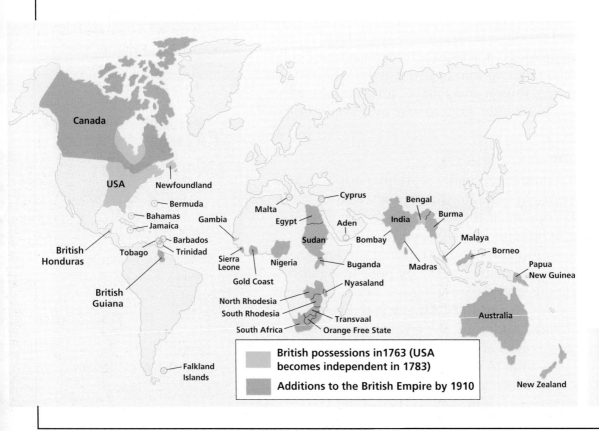

British possessions in 1763 (USA becomes independent in 1783)

Additions to the British Empire by 1910

The British Empire in 1763 and 1910.

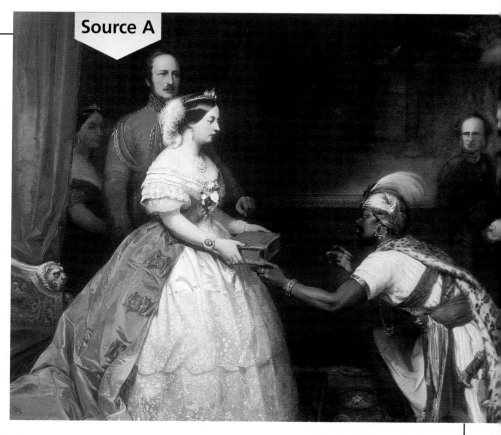

Source A

Queen Victoria presenting a bible to a foreign prince.

So men such as Cecil Rhodes and David Livingstone went to Africa believing that it was their duty to civilise the local population and teach them the benefits of the British way of life.

The spoils of war

In some ways the British Empire was gained almost by accident. Between 1700 and 1850 Britain won a number of wars which brought colonies as prizes for victory. For instance, Gibraltar was won in the War of Spanish Succession (1701–14). After defeating France and Austria in the Seven Years' War (1756–63), Britain gained Canada and parts of India. When the French Emperor Napoleon was defeated in the Napoleonic Wars in 1815, Britain gained Sri Lanka and parts of South Africa. Hong Kong became a British possession when China was defeated by Britain in the 'Opium Wars' of the nineteenth century.

Source B

A stuffed elephant at the Great Exhibition of 1851. This exhibition was set up to show the achievements of Britain in technology and engineering. Over 13,000 exhibits were put on show.

Branching out

Once the British realised the value of an empire, they were quite prepared to fight to keep territories or to gain new ones. So wars of conquest were fought in places such as South Africa, India and Egypt. Other places were gained more easily. Sir Stamford Raffles landed at Singapore in 1819 and negotiated an agreement with the local Sultan to let him build a British base there. In 1770 the explorer James Cook claimed Australia and New Zealand as British possessions and in the 1820s, 3000 convicts a year were being transported to work in Australia.

But Australia was an exception. Other British people who went to live in the Empire were not convicts. They ranged from administrators sent by the government, to merchants realising that the Empire provided an opportunity for making money to those who were attracted by the opportunity to 'start again' in a different land. During the nineteenth century an estimated ten million people emigrated to different parts of the British Empire. Large numbers also went elsewhere in the world, especially to America.

How did having an empire affect trade?

The countries in the Empire were treated as British possessions and there were strict rules about trade. These countries were not allowed to sell their goods to other European countries and had to use British ships to carry their goods. Ports such as London, Liverpool and Bristol built huge docks to handle the trade with the colonies. British trade boomed, sometimes at the expense of trade in the colonies.

Source D

Lieutenant Horace Dorien-Smith explaining in a letter to his local British newspaper how he survived the Battle of Isandhlwana in 1879:

At about ten-thirty the Zulus were seen coming over the hills in thousands. They were in a semi-circle and must have covered several miles of ground. No one knows how many there were, but the general idea was 20,000. Well, to cut a long story short, in half an hour they were right up to camp with bullets flying all over the place. The Zulus nearly all had firearms and lots of ammunition. The place where they seemed thinnest was where we all made for. We had to charge through them and lots of our men were killed there.

Source C

A painting of the Battle of Isandhlwana in 1879. In this battle the Zulus of South Africa defeated the British army. William Gladstone, a leading British politician, complained that the British were fighting the Zulus for committing 'no other offence than their attempt to defend their homes, their wives and families against British artillery with their naked bodies'.

In 1815 India exported thirteen times as much cotton cloth to Britain as it imported. Then Britain put heavy taxes on this cloth. By 1832 British exports of cloth to India were sixteen times what India sold to Britain. The Indian cloth industry had been destroyed to help British cloth merchants.

British merchants also benefited from cheap raw materials from the colonies. Imported sugar, cotton, cocoa and tea were processed in British factories, then resold in Britain or exported to other countries. Goods from the Empire had an impact on the lives of many British people. Wheat came from Canada, and as steamships became more common, food was imported in refrigerated ships. Meat came from South America and dairy products from Australia and New Zealand. New 'exotic' foods, such as bananas and pineapples became common in Britain by 1900.

Another trade made some Britons a lot of money, as you will read in the next unit. Until the slave trade was abolished in the British Empire in 1807 there was a lot of money to be made in the miserable trade in human beings.

Things to do

1 List all the reasons that you can find on pages 8–11 for Britain gaining an empire in the eighteenth and nineteenth centuries.

2 Why were some people opposed to having an empire?

3 Source B (page 9) was a particularly popular exhibit at the Great Exhibition. Why do you think this was?

4 Look at Source C. Do you think that the artist was just painting the scene as it was, or is there a special message in the painting?

5 Do you think that Sources C and D support the criticisms made by William Gladstone? Explain your answer.

6 Using the information on pages 8–11, explain what effects having an empire had on Britain.

The amount Britain earned from its exports in 1850.

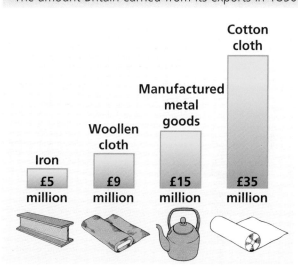

Iron £5 million
Woollen cloth £9 million
Manufactured metal goods £15 million
Cotton cloth £35 million

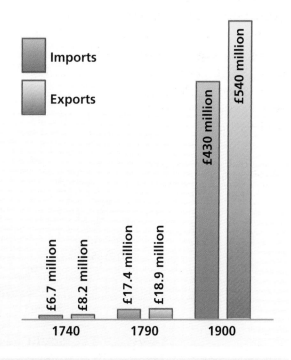

Imports
Exports

£6.7 million £8.2 million — 1740
£17.4 million £18.9 million — 1790
£430 million £540 million — 1900

British imports and exports 1740–1900.

1.2 THE SLAVE TRADE

What was the slave trade?

The slave trade was a trade in people, usually black people, from the west coast of Africa. These people were taken to the West Indies or America and sold to work on **plantations**. **Planters** grew sugar, coffee, tobacco and cotton to meet an ever-growing demand for these things in Britain. The more they could grow, the more money they could make. The British had traded slaves since the 1560s. By 1750 they had a very efficient system.

How did the system work?

Ships left Britain and sailed to West Africa. Here they swapped cloth, guns and alcohol for slaves. The slaves were then taken across the Atlantic to the West Indies. By 1750 there were specially designed ships, made to cram in as many slaves as possible. The conditions aboard these ships were appalling. The slaves were sold, mostly in the West Indies, although some were sold directly in America. Merchants then bought sugar, tobacco, coffee, rum and cotton with the money from selling slaves. They sailed back to Britain and sold these goods in Britain or in other parts of Europe.

Source A

From the Journal of Nicholas Owen, who set up as a slave trader in West Africa in the 1750s:

The people here trade elephant teeth [ivory tusks], slaves and rice for guns, gunpowder and shot, pewter, pans, brass kettles, iron bars and cloth. We purchase slaves for the merchants – a troublesome job. Some merchants dislike this trade, but not many. You have to give people drink and iron bars, then they get slaves for you. You still have to pay for the slaves. You can make enough when trade is quick, but when trade falls off, very few English ships come. Then the slaves pile up and their prices fall.

The slave trade was also known as the triangular trade. The map shows what was traded at each stopping point on the triangle.

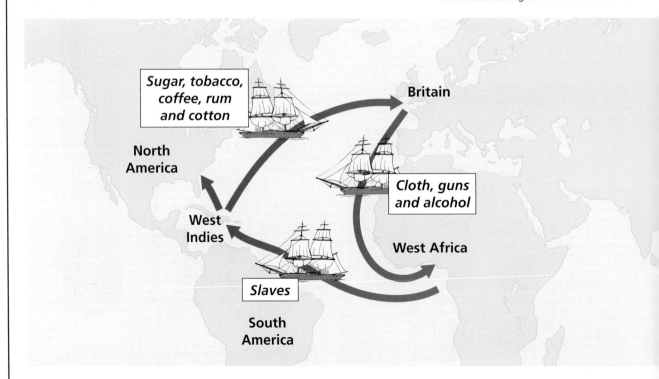

North America

Sugar, tobacco, coffee, rum and cotton

Britain

Cloth, guns and alcohol

West Indies

West Africa

Slaves

South America

Why was the slave trade important?

The slave trade made some merchant families very rich indeed. But it had an effect on the lives of many people who were not directly involved. Slavery made sugar, tobacco and cotton cheaper. More people could afford them. The slave trade helped Britain's trade abroad, because the British could sell their goods, especially cotton cloth, at a good price. Slave traders helped the British economy. They put money from their trade into cotton mills, railways, roads and canals.

Did slavery exist in Britain?

People thought of slavery as something that happened in the colonies. But slaves were bought and sold in Britain too. They were advertised in the papers, next to houses for rent or unwanted furniture. In the eighteenth century some were even made to wear iron collars or chains. Most, however, were treated more like toys than slaves. A little black boy, dressed in silks and a turban, became a rich lady's fashion accessory. Either way, they were not treated as people. They could be sold or simply thrown out, for being sullen or out of fashion, or just for growing up. But as demands for the abolition of the slave trade grew, and as more became known about the conditions slaves suffered, attitudes to slavery changed.

Changing attitudes to slavery.

Things to do

1 a Explain how the slave trade worked.
b How did the triangular trade make it easy for British people to ignore the suffering from which the money was made?

2 a List some of the ways that people were told about the evils of slavery.
b Design an anti-slavery poster. Do not use too many words. Make your point with a picture and caption about how using goods produced by slaves encourages the system.

Trading in misery

So who traded in slaves? There were several sorts of slave traders. The ones who made the most money from the trade were families who had plantations in the West Indies and owned slaves themselves. They often had several family members involved in the trade, and socialised and married into other families in the same business. In this way they lived in their own little bubble, cut off from the rising number of people in Britain who were **abolitionists** (wanted slavery abolished). But they did not ignore the criticism.

Justifying slavery

Rich slave traders wrote a great deal, in books and letters to the papers, telling people how the well-meaning interference of abolitionists sprang from a complete misunderstanding of the situation. They had never been to plantations, did not understand slavery (which was really *good* for black people) and did not understand black people. They also pointed out how bad abolition would be for British trade.

Source C

Ordinary people with savings that they wanted to increase also took part in the slave trade. In 1795 a Liverpool man wrote:

Almost every man in Liverpool is a merchant. Many of the small ships that carry but a hundred slaves are kitted out by lawyers, drapers, rope-makers, grocers, barbers and tailors, all hoping to make a profit on the voyage.

Source D

In 1788 the poet William Cowper summed up why people tried to ignore the evils of slavery.

**I admit I am shocked at the purchase of slaves,
And fear those who buy them and sell them are knaves;
What I hear of their hardships, their tortures, and groans,
Is almost enough to draw pity from stones!
I pity them greatly, but I must be mumm [quiet],
For how could we do without sugar and rum?**

Source B

Trading ports

Some ports grew into thriving cities on the profits of the slave trade. Liverpool and Hull, Bristol and Lancaster all grew quickly once the triangular trade was set up. As well as trade in sugar and crops from America and the West Indies, the ports also got a lot of work building and repairing boats for the trade.

Dodshon Foster was a merchant in Lancaster who was involved in the slave trade. Trading in slaves was a quick way to riches and to respectability. Several men who became rich from the slave trade in Lancaster also became mayors of the city.

THE LONG FAMILY

Samuel Long set up a sugar plantation in Jamaica when he arrived, aged 17, with the English army in 1655. When he died, in 1683, he left two plantations and possessions worth £12,000 – a great deal of money at the time.

Samuel's son, Charles, moved to England in 1700. This was a bad move. A friend wrote to Charles (in 1707) that his house in Jamaica needed repair, his crops were neglected, his slaves hardly fed – everything was falling apart. He said Charles should come back. He never did. He was making enough money anyway.

By this time other members of the family were running Jamaican plantations. One of these was Samuel Long II (nephew of the first Samuel Long). He had lands in Jamaica, Cornwall and London. His son Edward took over when he died in 1757. Edward was brought up in Britain. But he fitted in quickly in Jamaica. Family connections and his training in the law meant he became a judge in the courts, as well as a plantation owner. He married the only daughter of Thomas Beckford, the richest slave owner in Jamaica (grandson of a man who came to Jamaica in 1655, like Samuel Long). Edward Long is famous for his writings which defend plantation owning and slavery.

Long retired to England in 1769, because of ill-health. He had foolish ideas about the inferiority of black people. He wrote:

I think there are extremely good reasons for believing that the White and the Negro are two distinct species. Black people do not have hair, but a covering of wool. They have a bestial [animal like] smell. They have no plan or system of **morality**. *They are cruel to their children. When we look at their dissimilarity to the rest of mankind, must we not conclude that they are different? Indeed they have more in common with the orangutan.*

Source E

Milling sugar in Antigua. This illustration comes from a book about travels in the West Indies. It may be accurate about the process of milling sugar in the early 1800s, but the slaves are too well dressed, too unhurried, too clean and too well fed for the picture to be an accurate reflection of life on a sugar plantation.

Things to do

1 Why might a slave trader see Source E as a good advert for the slave trade?

2 Many people at the time saw how ridiculous Long's ideas were. But others clung to them. Why might the people listed below do this?
   • a slave trader
   • a sugar importer
   • a coffee house owner.

Black people in Britain

Slaves were mostly confined to overseas plantations. This did not mean that there were no black people in Britain. They came back with plantation owners who wanted to settle in Britain. They also came as sailors or as servants. Many arrived as slaves. Here are the experiences of just a few of them.

FRANCIS BARBER

Not all black servant-children were turned out of the house when they grew up (see page 13). Some became part of the family. Francis Barber was born a slave in Jamaica. In 1750, when he was still a boy, he came to Britain as Captain Bathurst's servant. Bathurst had Barber educated. When he died, in 1752, he gave Barber his freedom. Barber went to work for Dr Johnson, a friend of Bathurst. Johnson let Barber carry on with his education. He let him get married in 1776. When Johnson died, in 1782, he left Barber all his property. Barber and his wife set up a school in Staffordshire which they ran until Barber died in 1801. His wife then ran the school alone.

Runaways

People put adverts in newspapers asking for help in tracking down runaway slaves:

Hannah Press, a serving maid of middle height and brown complexion, wearing a light gown and petticoat and a dark riding hood, speaking broad Yorkshire, ran away from service Sunday, 2 March. She took with her a silver tankard, a silver plate, six silver forks, six silver spoons.

John Bowman, apprentice to John Ibbett, ran away from his master Monday last. He is about 19 years of age, brown complexion about 5' 3" high. He has a sullen look and wears a dark brown wig and a blue coat.

Run away from his master, a Negro boy, under five feet high, about 16 years old. Named Charles. He is bow-legged, hollow-backed and pot-bellied.

Steps to freedom in Britain

1772 Slaves cannot be taken out of Britain against their will.
1807 Slave trade abolished.
1833 Slavery abolished in British colonies.

Source F

In the 1750s it was very fashionable to have black children as servants, as this painting shows.

JAMES SOMERSET

James Somerset came to Britain in 1769. He was brought as a slave by his American master, Charles Stewart. In 1771 he ran away. He hid in London's free black community. Stewart tracked Somerset down. He had him kidnapped and given to the captain of the ship *Ann and Mary*, which was due to sail for Jamaica. He told the captain to lock Somerset up, take him to Jamaica and sell him.

Granville Sharp, who was one of the earliest British abolitionists, heard about the case. He wanted to bring the case to law. He said he needed Somerset as a witness, so he could not be taken from the country. The case was taken to court, under the argument that, while the colonies accepted slavery, it was not part of British law. So, the defence lawyer said, once slaves set foot on English soil they were under British law, and free. The judge, Lord Mansfield, tried hard to make people settle the case out of court. He was under a lot of pressure: *I am told there are no less than 15,000 slaves now in England, who will desire their liberty if the law decides in favour of this case. This will cost their owners some £700,000. Yet if we allow ourselves to be ruled by the laws of the colonies, the implications are yet worse.* On 22 June 1772, Mansfield gave his decision: *Slavery was never in use in this country. It is so odious that it cannot be supported on moral, or political grounds. Whatever inconvenience may follow from this decision, the black man is freed.* We know that Somerset was freed, but not what happened to him after.

Fears and rumours.

Things to do

1 **a** Why was the Somerset case a good thing for black people?
  b What problems might it have caused black people?

2 What evidence on these pages would you use to show that black people were badly treated in Britain?

3 What evidence on these pages would you use to show that black people were well treated in Britain?

During the eighteenth century the British began to take an interest in trade with India. Indian goods such as textiles, **indigo** and spices could be sold at a good profit in Britain. A group of merchants formed the East India Company, which was given sole rights to trade in India by the British government. In return, the East India Company agreed to give the British government a share of its profits.

The French also formed an East India Company and the two rival companies were forced to have their own small army to protect their trade in India. Then in 1756 Britain and France went to war. The French encouraged the ruler of Bengal, Nawab Saraj ud-Daulah, to attack the British base at Calcutta. What happened next has become part of British history, but no one is really sure how true it is.

The Hole

The story goes that in 1756 Saraj ud-Daulah attacked and captured the English settlement at Calcutta. He imprisoned 146 English prisoners in a notorious military prison which was only about 8 metres by 6 metres. The room was so small and so short of air that by the next morning 123 of the prisoners had died. The story of the 'Black Hole of Calutta' appeared in British children's history books for much of the eighteenth and nineteenth centuries.

There are, however, one or two problems with the story. It comes from the writings of a survivor, John Holwell, who was a British official in the area. Holwell describes how, as soon as the prisoners were thrust into the small room, they began to sweat profusely and soon developed a raging thirst. It was not long before everyone was 'giving way to the violence of their passions' and fighting each other, even killing people, in an effort to get to the one small window. Indian historians have since carried out investigations into the episode. They believe that the numbers killed in the prison were much lower, or even that the event never took place at all.

Some interesting facts about the Black Hole of Calcutta

- The prison was already called the 'Black Hole' before the events of 1756.
- An Indian history book written a few years after the event lists attacks on the English by Indians, but does not mention the Black Hole of Calcutta.
- No report of the event was ever made to the Directors of the East India Company.
- In 1757 leaders from Britain and India signed the Treaty of Alingar in which the Indians agreed to pay compensation for attacks on British citizens. No mention was made of the Black Hole of Calcutta.

A cartoon version of the Black Hole published in a recent British school history book.

12 MEANWHILE, IN INDIA: Another Indian prince, Suraj-ud-Dowlah, tried to drive out the East India Company. On 20 June 1756, he captured Calcutta in the north of India, and threw 146 Britons into prison.

13 **Source A**

WATER, FOR GOD'S SAKE!

THE BLACK HOLE OF CALCUTTA
Shut all night in a tiny room, without water, all but 23 of the 146 Britons died.

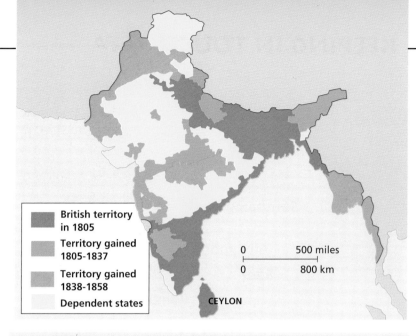

The establishment of British control in India 1757–1900.

ROBERT CLIVE

Robert Clive's victory at Plassey has earned him the title 'The Father of India'. Following his victory he returned to England in 1760 and, using money he received from gifts and bribes in India, he bought himself a seat as an MP. He was made a baron in 1764 and returned to India to become Governor of Bengal. Ill-health led him to return to England in 1773, where his opponents arranged an investigation into his behaviour in India, accusing him of '**plundering** Bengal'. He was **acquitted**, but the disgrace, coupled with an addiction to opium, led him to take his own life in 1775.

Defeat for the Nawab

Whether or not there is any truth in the story of the Black Hole of Calcutta, Nawab Saraj ud-Dauluh did not profit from his attack on Calcutta. On 23 June 1757, Robert Clive led a force of the East India Company against the Nawab at a small village called Plassey. The so-called 'battle' lasted only a few hours and its outcome was decided before the armies met. Most of the Nawab's army had been bribed to change sides and he was easily defeated. Saraj ud-Dauluh's body was found in a nearby river a few days later.

India becomes a British colony

Following the victory at Plassey, the British steadily gained more control of India and by 1763 the French had been driven from the country. During the next century Britain took control of much of India. After a mutiny by Indian soldiers in the British army in 1857, the British government decided to take direct control of the country instead of allowing the East India Company to run affairs. In 1877 Queen Victoria was given the title Empress of India and a **Viceroy** was put in charge of the government of India. India's wealth was so important to Britain that India has often been referred to as 'the jewel in the crown' of the British Empire.

India remained a British possession until it was given its independence in 1947. This independence, however, came only after a long campaign by people like Mahatma Gandhi and after determined efforts by the British to stop protests against their rule, such as at Amritsar.

Things to do

1 Why did Britain want to control India?

2 a Where do you think the story of the Black Hole of Calcutta came from?

  b Why do you think it appeared in British school history books throughout the nineteenth century?

  c What evidence is there to suggest that the story is not true?

3 Write a letter from an Indian historian explaining why you think the British version of the story is not true.

How did Britain keep in touch with its growing empire? For much of the period we are studying there was only one answer – letters. From 1850 one of the fastest ways to carry things around the world was on the new steamships. One of the companies set up to take letters, and passengers, all over the Empire was the Peninsular and Oriental Steam Navigation Company – P & O for short. The P & O competed with other companies to carry government mail, soldiers and almost anything else!

- Southampton
- Alexandria
- Suez
- Calcutta
- Hong Kong
- Bombay
- *Red Sea*
- Singapore
- Sidney
- Melbourne

Overland route between Alexandria and Suez (before the Suez canal existed).

Frank Kendall

Frank Kendall joined P & O in 1856, aged 17. He worked at the Southampton office for two years. In 1858 he was sent to Bombay and then Calcutta, Singapore, Hong Kong and Melbourne. Kendall married in 1867 and had six sons and a daughter. He returned to London in 1881. Kendall retired in 1906 and died a year later. All but one of his sons spent most of their lives working abroad. One of them, Herbert, worked for P & O. Opposite are extracts from just a few of Frank Kendall's letters home, written in 1858 and 1859.

The places where Frank Kendall worked for P & O.

The *Great Eastern* steam ship, which laid the first telegraph cable under the Atlantic.

Things to do

You are a historian preparing work on Frank Kendall. Write an account of what we learn from his letters about:

- the problems P & O faced
- new inventions
- the dangers of travel
- living abroad
- Frank Kendall as a person.

Source A

Extract 1
1858: From Southampton to Bombay

17 February: We made it to Gibraltar in just under five days. The soldiers have plenty of room. Many ships this size would cram in 700 or 800 soldiers, but we only have 250. The boat has been **pitching.** The ducks do not like it and quack loudly. They are seasick and get thinner each meal. Sheep are much better passengers.

28 February: We arrived at Alexandria and went to Suez with the troops by train. At the end of the railway we went the 25 miles to Suez by donkey.

9 March: We arrived at Aden to hear the Ava was lost, along with the Calcutta mail. The ship was worth £70,000. P & O will have to pay for the lost cargo. She was also bringing a new shaft for the Alma, which will have to wait for another one and spend even longer laid up. But the Company loses only about three ships a year and hardly any lives lost at all.

18 March: We arrived in Bombay the night before last. I went to the office yesterday and was put to work at once. Very busy.

Extract 2
1858: Working in Bombay

20 March: There are three others in the office with me and about a dozen native workers. I went to the docks and met the Electric Telegraph people, who say it should not be hard to lay cable through the Red Sea, then we will be able to speak to England in a matter of hours!

23 March: I share a house with 3 others. My servant can speak no English. I speak little Hindustani. But he is said to be good. Servants here do not cheat their masters, but the natives will, in general, never tell the truth if they can lie.

19 June: The drainage in Bombay is awful. When the monsoon rains come, the streets are one big sewer. There are people who are supposed to make sure the streets are cleared, but they don't do it. Cholera, dysentery and fever are all rife. Everything gets damp and mouldy in this weather; except for the metal – which goes rusty!

Extract 3
1859: Suez and Australia

In 1859 Frank was sent, as a **Purser**, from Bombay to Australia via Suez, to learn more about how P & O ships were run.

28 March: At Suez. The passengers transferring to our ship came, with much grumbling about delays, gales and missing luggage. At last we got everything stowed and sailed. One morning there was a cry of 'Man overboard!' The ship stopped. The poor fellow was just visible, some three miles off. By the time the lifeboat got there he was gone. Sharks, probably.

21 April: At Aden. The Emeu had a broken shaft. The Granada will take the mail and passengers – they will reach England a week or more late. We left with 240 tons of coal, in every corner and all over the deck, for the long leg of our journey.

14 May: Sydney harbour is beautiful. Sydney and Melbourne have fine buildings, very fine shops and markets where things are much cheaper than in Bombay. They have a real 'go-ahead' feel. Australia is a wonderful country. I would go there tomorrow, if P & O asked me. But I do not wish to become a Purser; it is not the life for me.

12 July: I see the Telegraph is now laid to Aden. So you will hear of our return to Bombay before you get this letter.

Kendall returned to Bombay on 10 September. He was sent to Singapore (the Telegraph followed him!) then Hong Kong in 1863 and Bombay in 1864. He eventually got his wish to live in Australia. He was sent to Melbourne in 1865, where he stayed till he retired.

In the sixteenth century the English government began transporting persistent beggars to the colonies overseas. In the reign of Charles II this practice was extended to include criminals of all kinds. A sentence of transportation to the American colonies meant that such people were 'out of harm's way'.

But in 1783 the American colonies won their independence from Britain and so a new dumping ground for criminals had to be found. An ideal place soon emerged. In 1770 James Cook had landed on the Australian coastline at Botany Bay, claimed it for Britain and renamed it 'New South Wales'.

Source A

Punishments received for various crimes at Gloucester Assizes in 1826.

William James: for breaking into a house and stealing 20 pounds of cheese: 7 years' transportation.
Thomas James: for house-breaking and stealing shirts etc.: Death.
George Cooke: for house-breaking and stealing a quilt: 7 years' transportation.
James Turner: For robbing J. Underwood of a hat on the highway: Death.
Sarah Mears: for receiving 24 bottles of wine knowing them to be stolen: 14 years' transportation.
William Chivers: for breaking into a house and stealing 21 cheeses: 7 years' transportation.
Richard Mee: for stealing a bottle of brandy: 7 years' transportation.
George Goode: for killing T. Hawkins: 18 months' imprisonment.
Elizabeth Jones: for stealing calico and other crimes: Transportation for life.
Richard Fowler: for stealing hay: 12 months' imprisonment.

Cook reported that the new continent was suitable for 'hardy pioneers' to settle and the British Prime Minister, William Pitt, decided to set up a colony of convicts at Botany Bay.

First arrivals

The first fleet of ships, carrying 759 convicts (568 men and 191 women) together with 200 **marines** to guard them, arrived at Botany Bay in January 1788. Captain Arthur Phillip described Botany Bay as 'a poor and sandy heath full of swamps' and so landed further up the coast. Here on 26 January (now known as Australia Day) he began to build a settlement, which he named 'Sydney' after the Home Secretary, Lord Sydney.

It seems strange to think that what is today a mighty nation was for many years known in Britain merely as a **penal colony** for unwanted convicts. Between 1788 and 1868, when transportation ended, about 150,000 convicts were transported to New South Wales, Western Australia and Van Diemen's Land (modern-day Tasmania).

Not all dangerous criminals

The convicts transported to Australia were not all serious criminals. Some were convicted of nothing more than petty crimes, such as stealing cheese or handkerchiefs. Others were well-educated and wealthy people who had committed crimes such as forgery. Some 20% of those transported were women, many of them prostitutes. There was also a large number of Irish people, banished from their homeland after an uprising against the British in 1798. There were also 'political prisoners' whose beliefs had landed them in trouble. Perhaps the best known of these were the Tolpuddle Martyrs, whom you will read about on pages 24–5.

A nineteenth-century drawing showing convicts being transported to Australia.

But many of those transported to Australia were very poor, with little education and few skills. This explains the appalling treatment they received during the crossing and on arrival. In 1790 the *Neptune* set sail with 502 convicts, of whom 158 died before they reached Australia. The government was forced to pay a bonus on future voyages for each convict safely landed to make sure treatment improved. Even so, treatment was harsh; prisoners were always shackled and **floggings** were common. In Australia conditions could be almost as bad. Flogging was a common penalty with up to 200 lashes being given for theft. Individual convicts were assigned to private employers who often treated them as slaves. However, for some enterprising convicts with a sympathetic master there was the opportunity to 'start again' and make a success of their lives.

Source C

The story of James Pollock, transported to Van Diemen's Land and sent to work for a cruel master.

I did not know what to do; I walked away from the house. My master took up a loaded gun and followed me and swore that he would shoot me if I did not come back. I still went on, for at the time I did not care whether he shot me or not.

The next day I was reported as missing and after four days in the bush with nothing to eat I was captured by a constable. When I appeared before the magistrate my master said how well he treated me and what an idle fellow I was. So the magistrate sentenced me to fifty lashes.

I was then sent back and my master put me to work carrying logs on my back. He was more cruel than ever and I was determined not to stay with him. I ran away four times and got fifty lashes each time.

Finally I was sentenced to fifty lashes more, three months working on the chain gang and then to go back to my master. When I was tied to the triangle to be lashed, my back was in such a mess that the doctor told them to flog me across my breeches.

The Tolpuddle Martyrs

On a cold, grey February morning in 1834, in the tiny Dorset village of Tolpuddle, George Loveless strode out vigorously to his work down the village street, quite unaware of the cruel fate that awaited him. It came in the shape of the parish constable, who on that fateful morning was required to undertake the distasteful duty of arresting his friend and neighbour, George.

The constable stopped him. 'I have a warrant from the magistrates for your arrest, Mr Loveless.'

'For me?'

'Yes, and for others beside you: James Hammett, Thomas Standfield and his son John, young Brine and for your brother, James.'

'What is the warrant for?' asked Loveless. 'What have we done?'

'You'd best take it and read for yourself' was the reply.

Loveless read the warrant, which charged him and his companions with having participated in the taking of an illegal oath. At the request of the constable, Loveless accompanied him to the cottages of the other men. Then the six of them, in the custody of the constable, marched towards the dreadful ordeal which awaited them at the end of the seven miles' walk to Dorchester.

Source D

CAUTION.

WHEREAS it has been represented to us from several quarters, that mischievous and designing Persons have been for some time past, endeavouring to induce, and have induced, many Labourers in various Parishes in this County, to attend Meetings, and to enter into Illegal Societies or Unions, to which they bind themselves by unlawful oaths, administered secretly by Persons concealed, who artfully deceive the ignorant and unwary,—WE, the undersigned Justices think it our duty to give this PUBLIC NOTICE and CAUTION, that all Persons may know the danger they incur by entering into such Societies.

ANY PERSON who shall become a Member of such a Society, or take any Oath, or assent to any Test or Declaration not authorized by Law—

Any Person who shall administer, or be present at, or consenting to the administering or taking any Unlawful Oath, or who shall cause such Oath to be administered, although not actually present at the time—

Any Person who shall not reveal or discover any Illegal Oath which may have been administered, or any Illegal Act done or to be done—

Any Person who shall induce, or endeavour to persuade any other Person to become a Member of such Societies,

WILL BECOME

Guilty of Felony,

AND BE LIABLE TO BE

Transported for Seven Years.

ANY PERSON who may be compelled to take such an Oath, unless he shall declare the same within four days, together with the whole of what he shall know touching the same, will be liable to the same Penalty.

Any Person who shall directly or indirectly maintain correspondence or intercourse with such Society, will be deemed Guilty of an Unlawful Combination and Confederacy, and on Conviction before one Justice, on the Oath of one Witness, be liable to a Penalty of TWENTY POUNDS; or to be committed to the Common Gaol or House of Correction, for THREE CALENDAR MONTHS; or if proceeded against by Indictment, may be CONVICTED OF FELONY, and be TRANSPORTED FOR SEVEN YEARS.

Any Person who shall knowingly permit any Meeting of any such Society to be held in any House, Building, or other Place, shall for the first offence be liable to the Penalty of FIVE POUNDS; and for every other offence committed after Conviction, be deemed Guilty of such Unlawful Combination and Confederacy, and on Conviction before one Justice, on the Oath of one Witness, be liable to a Penalty of TWENTY POUNDS, or to be committed to the Common Gaol or House of Correction, FOR THREE CALENDAR MONTHS; or if proceeded against by Indictment may be

CONVICTED OF FELONY,

And Transported for SEVEN YEARS.

COUNTY OF DORSET,
Dorchester Division.

C. B. WOLLASTON,
JAMES FRAMPTON,
WILLIAM ENGLAND,
THOS. DADE,
JNO. MORTON COLSON.

HENRY FRAMPTON,
RICHD. TUCKER STEWARD,
WILLIAM R. CHURCHILL,
AUGUSTUS FOSTER.

February 22d, 1834.

G. CLARK, PRINTER, CORNHILL, DORCHESTER.

The notice issued by Dorchester magistrates two days before the arrest of the Tolpuddle Martyrs.

This account of the arrest of six Dorsetshire farm labourers comes from a book published by the Trades Union Congress (TUC) in 1934. To the TUC the labourers were heroes and the book itself is called 'The book of the **Martyrs** of Tolpuddle'. But it is not just the TUC which thinks so highly of the men. Historians also call them 'The Tolpuddle Martyrs'. Who were they, and why are they considered martyrs?

In the early nineteenth century, conditions for many agricultural labourers were appalling. (You can read more about this in the section on the 'Captain Swing' riots, on page 89). It was not uncommon for families of eleven persons to live in a one-roomed cottage just three metres square. Wages were about ten shillings (50p) a week and the standard of living was so low that farm labourers were said to live on 'tea and potatoes'.

Wages in the Tolpuddle area were nine shillings (45p) a week and the local labourers, led by George Loveless, asked for a rise to ten shillings. The farm owners refused and to teach the labourers a lesson they reduced wages first to eight shillings (40p) and then to seven shillings (35p). The men decided to form a trade union to protect themselves. In October 1833 they set up 'The Friendly Society of Agricultural Labourers'. New members of the union had to go through a joining ceremony and swear an oath of allegiance to the union.

It was not illegal to join a trade union, but the authorities disliked working people joining together. It was only a few years since there had been a revolution in France and mutinies in the British navy. So when local magistrates heard about the Tolpuddle union they wrote to the Home Secretary, Lord Melbourne, to ask for advice. He told them to use the law banning people from taking 'illegal oaths' – passed in 1797 to stamp out the navy mutiny.

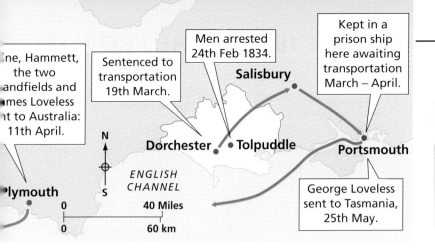

Men arrested 24th Feb 1834.

Sentenced to transportation 19th March.

Kept in a prison ship here awaiting transportation March – April.

ne, Hammett, the two andfields and mes Loveless t to Australia: 11th April.

Salisbury

Dorchester • **Tolpuddle**

Portsmouth

N

S

ENGLISH CHANNEL

lymouth

0   40 Miles

0   60 km

George Loveless sent to Tasmania, 25th May.

The arrest and transportation of the Tolpuddle Martyrs.

The local magistrates announced that taking an oath to join a union was illegal. Two days later they arrested Loveless and his five colleagues. The men had not known they were breaking the law when they took their oath, but they were found guilty and on 19 March were sentenced to seven years' transportation.

To Australia

On 27 March five of the labourers (George Loveless was too ill to travel) were taken in chains to a prison ship in Portsmouth Harbour. They were transferred to a convict ship and on 11 April set sail for Australia. On 17 August, after a voyage of 111 days, they arrived at Sydney Harbour. They remained on board for three weeks before going to convict barracks in the town. From there they were sent to carry out their seven years of hard labour.

George Loveless was better by 5 April, but he did not join the others. He was taken in chains to Portsmouth and on 25th May set sail for Van Diemen's Land (Tasmania), 700 miles from where his colleagues had been sent.

Pardon and return

The sentence passed on the Tolpuddle Martyrs was very unpopular in Britain and there were many protest meetings. Lawyers and some MPs criticised the judge and said that the conviction was not legal. On 21 April 1834 more than 50,000 people marched in protest in London. In June the new Home Secretary, Lord John Russell, offered to give pardons to four of the men after two years (but not George and James Loveless, who were considered ringleaders). Eventually, in March 1836, the government gave a free pardon to all six men. Even then it was almost a year before they came home and two years before James Hammett was found and returned to Tolpuddle. He remained in Tolpuddle for the rest of his life. The other five emigrated to Canada in 1844 to start a new life.

Source E

From a speech made by George Loveless at the trial:

My Lord, if we have violated any law, it was not done intentionally; we have injured no man's reputation, character, person or property; we were uniting together to preserve ourselves, our wives and our children from utter degradation and starvation. We challenge any man to prove that this is not the case.

Things to do

1 How can you tell that the writer of the account on page 24 was sympathetic to the Tolpuddle labourers?

2 Look at Source D. What grounds do people have for saying that the conviction was not legal?

3 George Loveless was sent to a different area from the other labourers. Why do you think that was?

4 Write a speech for an MP to give in Parliament, either complaining about or supporting the treatment of the Tolpuddle Martyrs.

5 Why do you think the Tolpuddle Martyrs have become so important in history?

Landlords

Most of the land in Ireland was owned by landlords who lived in England. They rarely, if ever, visited their estates. Some landlords did live in Ireland but, instead of investing money in their land, spent it on good living in Dublin. A few landlords tried to do their best for their tenants. But tenants could only afford low rents, and this did not bring in enough money for landlords to improve the land.

Population and land

Between 1821 and 1841 the population of Ireland increased from 6.8 million to 8.2 million. There was enormous competition for land. Tenant farmers, who rented their land from the landowners, **sub-let** to more and more labourers. Hundreds of families tried to live off plots of land which were too small to make a profit; they just about supported the family – if they were lucky.

Crops

Most Irish people lived on unimproved land which was wet and soggy. There they grew the only crop they could – the potato. And they lived on it. A diet of milk and potatoes was enough to keep them healthy, provided the crop was good. There were areas of more fertile land where corn was grown, but the corn was for selling, not eating. Without this income the Irish people could not pay the rent.

Famine!

In the spring of 1845 a deadly virus spread among the growing potatoes. When they were dug up, one in three was diseased by **blight**. Famine was a very real possibility for the 4 million people who depended on potatoes to live. The corn survived, but if the tenants did not pay the rent, they would be **evicted**. So it was best to go hungry and sell the corn. Boat load after boat load of corn sailed off to be sold in England. Everything depended on the next year's potato crop.

Source A

From The Condition of the Working Class in England by F. Engels, 1844. Despite the title, he is writing about the Irish in Ireland.

They have potatoes half enough for thirty weeks in the year, and the rest nothing. When the time comes in the spring when this food reaches its end, wife and children go to beg. Meanwhile the husband goes in search of work either in Ireland or England, and returns at the potato harvest to his family. This is the condition in which nine-tenths of the Irish country folks live.

This engraving shows how Irish labourers lived before the Famine.

Source B

Many people had been forced to eat their **seed potatoes**, but even so there were enough to plant about two-thirds of the normal quantity. But many diseased tubers had been planted and the spring was mild and damp. Blight spread again. Field after field turned black with rotting potatoes. The entire crop failed. The threat of famine had become a reality.

Disease

With famine came disease. When people are starving, ordinary diseases, like 'flu and measles, become killers. Scurvy was common. When people have scurvy their teeth drop out and their legs turn black because of burst blood vessels. The most serious disease of all was typhus. Typhus victims have a high fever, rashes and sores, swollen, blackened faces – and they smell awful. The Irish called typhus 'famine fever' and most people abandoned anyone who caught it. In 1846 typhus reached **epidemic** proportions. About one million Irish died in the Famine. Almost 90% of them died not from starvation but from disease.

An Irish funeral during the Famine.

Source D

Things to do

1 Read Source A and look at Source B.
  a What do they tell you about the way of life of Irish farm labourers?
  b What else would you want to know in order to write a full account of their lives?

2 Make a list of reasons for the Irish Famine. Explain why each of them contributed to the famine.

3 Why did so many people die during the Famine?

4 Why was so much good food exported from Ireland when half the population was starving?

5 Source D was published in the *Illustrated London News*. This paper was read by educated and wealthy people in England. For what reasons might the editor have wanted to print a picture of the funeral of an Irish labourer?

Since Ireland was part of the United Kingdom, people expected the British government to provide a solution to the problem of famine.

Relief Committees

Each district in Ireland had a Relief Committee of poor-law guardians, clergymen, teachers and magistrates, both Catholic and Protestant. Their job was to do their best to see people had the help they needed.

Cheap maize

The government spent £100,000 on maize from the USA. It was shipped to huge **depots** in Limerick and Cork and then distributed to smaller ones around the country. There were two main problems. Firstly, there were some parts of Ireland where these government depots were the only source of food, and they were besieged by starving people. Secondly, the maize was very difficult to grind into flour; Irish people had never cooked maize or eaten it before, so they made it into a kind of porridge. They hated it and called it 'Peel's **Brimstone**' because it was bright yellow and Robert Peel was the Prime Minister responsible for ordering the supply of cheap maize. But the Irish ate 'Peel's Brimstone'. They had no choice.

Public works

The government organised hundreds of road-building schemes so that starving people could work and earn money. Ireland didn't actually need the roads; Ireland needed land improvement schemes so that food could be grown. But the government wouldn't fund these because to do so would have meant using public money to benefit private landowners. By February 1847, 700,000 people were employed in road-making. This was costing a great deal and the government stopped all such schemes by June 1847.

Emigration

Another, more terrible 'solution' was found. By the time of the third year of famine, 1848, government help and sympathy were running thin. Irish landlords were forced to do what they could. They were themselves facing ruin. Their tenants had paid no rent for years. They couldn't improve their land and they couldn't make any profit from it. So they set about clearing tenants off their land and letting it in larger parcels to people who could pay.

Where were the poverty-stricken tenants to go? Some simply starved. Others decided to try their luck overseas. How did they pay for their passage? The cost of a passage was roughly the same as the cost of keeping a pauper in the workhouse for six months. So many poor law guardians and landlords paid the fares of families willing to go to the USA or Canada. It was cheaper that way. Others had their passage paid for by various charitable committees set up in Ireland and England.

Source A

Many ordinary people in England did what they could to help. Some formed committees and knitted, sewed and held fêtes to raise money for the starving Irish. Some, like this Quaker, William Bennett, went to Ireland with bales of clothes and sacks of turnip and flax seed to give away. Here he writes about the effect of soup kitchens. Usually they didn't serve soup at all, but a thick porridge called 'stirabout' made from maize flour or oatmeal.

At Tencurry and Turbid 3200 quarts (3635 litres) of porridge were distributed daily, to upwards of 800 families, one of the boilers being filled four or five times. The amount of distress ended in this way is impossible to calculate, and was seen in the improved appearance of the poor people since the soup kitchens had been in action.

Source B

By 1851 about one million Irish people had died from starvation and disease and another million had emigrated. Half the population of Ireland simply wasn't there any more.

In 1848 the British Parliament gave money to Irish **workhouses** and supplied them with cheap maize. In this picture, starving people are besieging an Irish workhouse, desperately trying to get food.

Source C

Sir William Butler, an Irish soldier and author, described what he had seen as a boy.

One day I was taken by my father to the scene of an eviction. On one side of the road was a ruined church; on the other side stood some dozen houses which were to be pulled down. At a signal from the sheriff the work began. The miserable inmates were dragged out upon the road; the thatched roofs were torn down and the earthen walls battered in by crowbars; the screaming women, the half-naked children, the paralysed grandmother and the tottering grandfather were hauled out. I was twelve years old at that time; but I think if a loaded gun had been put into my hands I would have fired into that crowd of villains as they plied their horrid trade by the ruined church of Tampul-da-voun.

Things to do

1 Make a list of all the 'solutions' people found for the starving Irish people.
  Which 'solution' would you have preferred if you were:
  a a starving labourer
  b an Irish landlord
  c a British politician?

2 Read Source C.
  The people were clearly very poor and were not making a good living from the land.
  a Why, then, were they desperate to stay in their home?
  b Why were their landlords equally desperate to get them out?
  Use what you know about Ireland at this time to explain your answer.

In the period covered by this book there was a major change in the way that Britain earned its living. In the mid-eighteenth century Britain was still an agricultural country. Most of its six million inhabitants lived in villages or small towns and earned their living working on the land. By modern standards there was only one town of any size, London, with a population of over half a million. Britain's major industry was the making of woollen cloth. But this did not generally happen in factories. Instead, spinning and weaving were done in the home under what historians have called the Domestic System.

Changes through power

There were some small factories in eighteenth-century Britain, though the lack of a reliable source of power meant that they had to rely on water-wheels to turn their machines. But at the beginning of the century one invention led to such dramatic changes in the way goods were produced that we now talk of an 'Industrial Revolution'. In 1698 steam was used to drive a pump to remove water from tin mines in Cornwall. In the next hundred years improvements to this 'steam engine' meant that it could be used to drive machinery in a factory. Now that there was a reliable source of power, factories sprang up and Britain began its Industrial Revolution. The factories, however, were mostly in the north of England, where coalfields provided fuel for the steam engines.

Source A

A steam engine built in 1778. Note how a series of cogs attached to the drive rod enable the engine to drive a wheel (see page 37). This was the basis on which trains were later to work.

Source B

Hebburn Colliery, County Durham, in 1844.

Source C

An engraving of a textile mill in Derby.

More factories meant more coal had to be produced to power the steam engines. Iron production had to increase to provide the materials for building steam engines and factories. The factories needed workers and so houses were built for them to live in. Soon towns with factories, or close to coalfields, began to develop into modern cities. Of course, people who lived in cities and worked in factories could not grow their own food, so farming had to change to produce more food for those who were unable to grow their own.

Workshop of the World

The Industrial Revolution led to Britain becoming the 'Workshop of the World', but this could not have happened without developments in transport. Raw materials had to reach factories, finished goods had to be transported to ports or markets in Britain, and food had to get to the cities. The rut-infested roads of eighteenth-century Britain could not do this – but the new canals, and later the railways, proved ideal!

Things to do

1 What was the 'Domestic System'?

2 Why were there so few factories in the early eighteenth century?

3 What was so important about the invention of an effective steam engine?

4 How do Sources A–D show the changes in Britain during the Industrial Revolution?

5 Do you agree that 'During the Industrial Revolution Britain became a totally different place'?

Source D

A painting from 1788 showing the country's first iron bridge. During the Industrial Revolution, iron manufacturers found a way to use coal-fired furnaces to turn iron ore into good-quality wrought iron, from which bridges could be built.

At the beginning of the eighteenth century more than half the population of England worked on the land or in a trade, such as milling, that was connected with agriculture. Most of the land was owned by rich **aristocrats** or gentry who rented it out to tenant farmers. These farmers paid labourers to work for them.

Strip farming

In much of England, farming used the 'open field' system, which involved dividing a village's fields into strips with every farmer having strips in each field. Every four years one of the village's fields was left fallow. That meant nothing was grown in it. Instead it was left to recover. As well as the fields which were cultivated there was also common land on which all villagers had the right to graze their livestock.

From the beginning of the eighteenth century, the population began to grow rapidly and more food was needed. This caused food prices to rise. Some farmers began to look at ways of growing more food and making more money.

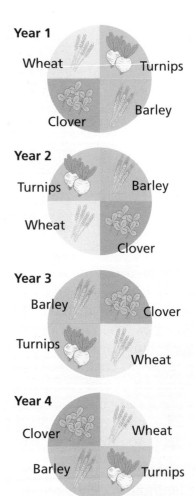

The Norfolk Rotation System ➤

Each crop extracts different nutrients from the soil, so they can be grown one after the other each year. Livestock can be put in the field of clover. As they eat, they also manure the fields.

Source A

A painting called 'The Haymakers' by George Stubbs. It was painted in 1786.

Source B

From a report on the *Sanitary Conditions of the Labouring Population of Great Britain*, 1842.

Most of the cottages are of the worst kind; some are mud hovels with piles of filth close to the doors. The mud floors of many are much below the level of the road and in wet seasons are little better than clay. Persons living in such cottages are generally very poor, very dirty and usually in rags, living almost wholly on bread and potatoes.

Enclosure

One way was to 'enclose' land – putting hedges round fields and farming them as one unit instead of in strips. As wealthy landowners began to enclose more and more land, they were able to use more efficient farming methods and needed fewer labourers. Some unscrupulous landowners also enclosed common land, so the ordinary farm labourers were doubly hit. Now they had nowhere to graze their own animals.

Farming techniques

Enclosure led to improvements in farming techniques. In Norfolk, a system of rotating crops, so that there was no need to rest the land for a year, helped boost production. This was also a time when new machinery began to be introduced into farming. A seed drill was invented to sow seed under the soil, ploughs became lighter so they were easier to use, and machines were used for separating the wheat from the **chaff**. This 'threshing' had previously been done by hand.

With enclosed fields, animals could be kept apart. This meant that not only were weak or diseased animals kept away from others, but farmers could select which animals to breed from. This selective breeding led to a vast increase in the size of livestock as farmers began breeding animals with shorter legs and larger bodies for more meat.

More efficient

The changes in agriculture brought great profits for landowners and farming became much more efficient. But many labourers lost their jobs, and there were periods when even the great landowners found it hard to make money from farming. As transport improved and refrigeration and canning were introduced, farmers also faced competition from abroad. This competition, together with a run of wet summers, led to terrible hardships in the 1870s. British farming had to become even more efficient before it could provide enough food at a cheap price for the country's industrial workers.

Things to do

1 What problems do you think the open field system might have caused for farmers?

2 Why was it necessary for farming to become more efficient?

3 What do you think would be the benefits and drawbacks of introducing enclosure?

4 What other improvements were made in agriculture at this time?

5 Look at Source A and read Source B.
How do you explain the difference between the workers painted in Source A and those described in Source B?

1710		1795
370 lb	Cattle	800 lb
70 lb	Calves	140 lb
28 lb	Sheep	80 lb
18 lb	Lambs	50 lb

Average weight of livestock at Smithfield market in 1710 and 1795.

THOMAS TURNER

Thomas Turner lived for most of his life in the Sussex village of East Hoathly. He was the village shop-keeper there – and very much more! We know the details of about eleven years of his life (1754–65) because he kept a diary. This tells us a lot, not only about Thomas' life, but about life in general in a small village in eighteenth-century England.

As you read these extracts from Thomas Turner's diary (in *italics*) and look at the other sources, work out what they tell you about Thomas Turner himself and what they tell you about life in his village and in eighteenth-century England.

Important dates in Thomas Turner's life

9 June 1729	Born at Groombridge, Kent.
June 1735	Family moved to Framfield, Sussex, where Thomas' father ran the village shop.
1750	Thomas rented a shop in East Hoathly, Sussex.
May 1752	Thomas' father died.
15 Oct 1753	Thomas married 20-year-old Peggy Slater. Their one child, a boy, died aged five months.
1 April 1759	Thomas' mother died.
23 June 1761	Thomas' wife died.
31 July 1765	Thomas married his second wife – Molly Hicks. They had one daughter and six sons, two of whom died when they were babies.
1766	Thomas bought his shop at East Hoathly, Sussex.
6 Feb 1793	Thomas Turner died and was buried in East Hoathley churchyard.

Shopkeeper

Mon 7 July 1755
Paid Halland the gardener 17 pence in full for cucumbers I sold for him.

Wed 24 Dec 1755
Paid John Jenner 21 shillings in payment for hats received from him today. In the evening wrote out Peter Adam's bill amounting to £8 16 shillings 1 pence. Gave 2 oz tobacco for two cheeses from Lewes.

Wed 1 Aug 1759
After breakfast rode over to Framfield and stayed there while my brother went to Uckfield to get me a pound of green tea, for which I paid him 9 shillings 3 pence.

Looking after the dead

Sat 8 March 1755
At the funeral of Mrs Piper. Gave out 20 pairs of men's and women's gloves.

Sat 27 Dec 1761
I set out for Lewes in order to get brass plates for Mr Calverley's coffin.

Sun 28 Dec 1761
In the morn I walked down to Whyly with a shroud, sheet etc. for Mr Calverley.

Teaching children

Thurs 13 Mar 1755
Mr Miller promised me his son should come to me to be taught.

Fri 20 June 1755
This day being my birthday I treated my scholars to about five quarts of strong beer.

Tues 17 June 1760
In the afternoon kept the school for Mr Long, he going to a cricket match at Chiddingly.

Helping the poor

Mon 22 Dec 1755

It being St Thomas' Day I gave to the poor of the parish, being about 30 in number, each one penny and a drink of beer.

Collecting taxes

Fri 9 Jan 1761

After breakfast went to Maresfield to meet the receiver-general of the land-tax, where I paid his clerk, Mr Thomas Gerry, the sum of £62 for half a year's land tax due from this parish.

● **Groombridge**

SUSSEX

Uckfield ● ● **Framfield**

● **East Hoathly**
● **Chiddingly**

● **Lewes**

● **Brighton**

N
S

0   10 Miles
0   14 km

Having fun

Thurs 27 May 1756

My wife and I went to Dicker Fair. We met with Miss Day and several more and I took them to a booth to treat them to a drink. I spent three shillings.

Sun 25 Dec 1757

This being Christmas Day the widow Marchant, Hannah Marchant and James Marchant dined with us on a buttock of boiled beef, a plum suet pudding and a pearl barley pudding, turnips and a wild plum pie.

Thurs 23 Feb 1758

During a wild party some of my friends poured into my room and made me put on my wife's petticoat. They made me dance with them without shoes or stockings until they had emptied their bottle of wine.

Source A

A modern photograph of Thomas Turner's cottage in East Hoathly.

Before steam

Before the development of steam power there were four main types of power used. None of them was totally satisfactory, as the cartoon below shows. Unreliable power sources meant factory owners could not always produce their goods. This in turn caused them to lose money. A more reliable form of power had to be found if the Industrial Revolution was to progress further. Steam was the answer.

The first British steam engine was developed in 1698 by Thomas Savery, who created the machine to pump water out of Cornish mines. However, it couldn't raise water above 20m, and was unreliable. It was dangerous, too, since the boilers were weak and often exploded. Little surprise, then, that it was replaced 14 years later by a much more effective machine, developed by Thomas Newcomen.

Thomas Newcomen

Newcomen grew up in Devon and knew the problems of the Cornish mines. He set about producing a better steam engine that could pump water up from 50m. However, this engine relied on a lot of coal, and there were no coalmines in Cornwall, so it was very expensive to run.

James Watt

In 1769, forty years after Newcomen's death, James Watt was asked by the University of Glasgow to repair a model Newcomen engine. Whilst working on it, Watt became aware of how fuel-hungry the engine was. So he set about finding ways to improve the engine to produce more power without using so much coal.

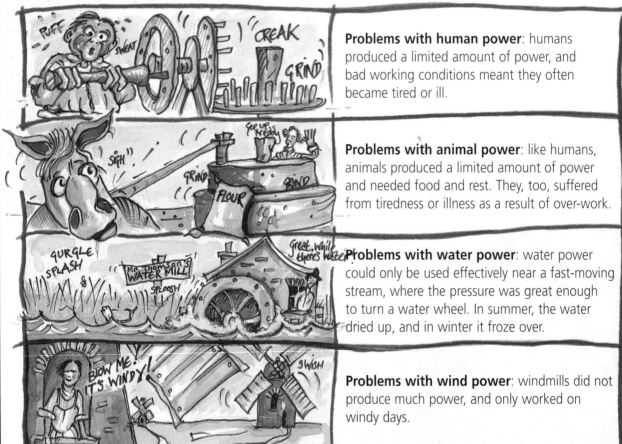

Problems with human power: humans produced a limited amount of power, and bad working conditions meant they often became tired or ill.

Problems with animal power: like humans, animals produced a limited amount of power and needed food and rest. They, too, suffered from tiredness or illness as a result of over-work.

Problems with water power: water power could only be used effectively near a fast-moving stream, where the pressure was great enough to turn a water wheel. In summer, the water dried up, and in winter it froze over.

Problems with wind power: windmills did not produce much power, and only worked on windy days.

Watt was so successful that his invention used only a quarter of the fuel needed by Newcomen's engine. Now factory owners began to look at the possibility of using the steam engine to drive their machines.

By 1776 Watt's first engine was being used in collieries. By now Watt had joined forces with Matthew Boulton, and they set about making a steam engine that could work in rotary motion, instead of just parallel (see below). This was achieved in 1781, and opened up many other industries to the reliability of steam power. It is not hard to see why the steam engine was one of the key developments of the Industrial Revolution.

By 1800 the industries that relied on steam power were wide and varied – from brewing to coin making, mining to sugar making. The cheap and reliable power produced by the new steam engines helped make Britain the most important manufacturing country in the world.

Source A

The writer James Boswell visited Boulton and Watt's factory in Soho. Boswell wrote this after the visit.

I shall never forget Mr Boulton's expression to me: 'I sell here, Sir, what all the world desires to have – power'.

This is a diagram of a typical 'sun and planet gear'. The driving rod (A) goes up and down (parallel motion), powered by the steam engine. At the end of the rod is a cog (B), which has teeth that slot into another cog in the middle of the wheel (C). As the teeth in the two cogs connect, the wheel is forced round, creating rotary motion.

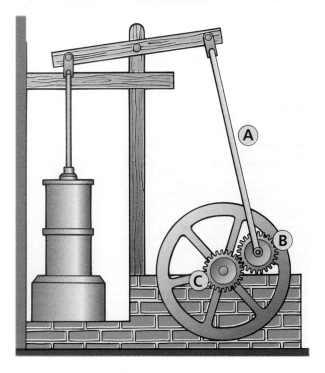

Source B

James Watt, painted in 1869.

Things to do

1 Why might a factory owner have had difficulty running his machines before the invention of an efficient steam engine?

2 Some historians call James Watt 'the father of the Industrial Revolution'. What do you think they mean?

2.5 LIVING AND WORKING CONDITIONS IN INDUSTRIAL BRITAIN

An increasing population

During the eighteenth and nineteenth centuries the population of Britain increased dramatically. From 1801 the government began to take a census (count) of the population every ten years, and from 1837 official records of births, marriages and deaths were kept. For the years before 1801 historians have had to make guesses about the population based on how many people were paying tax or how many were recorded in church parish registers as being baptised or buried.

What we can be sure of, however, is that the number of people in the country increased. By 1900 there were more than six times as many people living in Britain as there had been in 1750.

Historians are not really very sure about why this population increase happened. Obviously if more people are born than die, the population will increase. During the eighteenth century, the average age at which people married dropped from 27 to nearer 20, so families tended to be larger. As jobs for children became available in the new factories, people were less concerned about not being able to feed their families, so this may have helped too.

Things to do

1 How many more people were there in Britain in 1901 than in:
   a 1741
   b 1841?

2 What other useful information about population changes can you find in the bar graph on the opposite page?

3 How accurate is the evidence that historians have about population change at this time?

4 What point do you think the cartoonist in Source A was trying to make?

Source A

LONDON going out of Town. — or — The March of Bricks & Mortar!

A cartoon published in 1829 called 'The March of Bricks and Mortar'.

Of course, if families have more children, there are more people to have children in the future and so the population keeps increasing.

The death rate may also have decreased during this time. Although many families lived in appalling conditions in the new industrial towns, there were big improvements in medical care, particularly with the introduction of **inoculation** against killer diseases such as smallpox. Many families were also eating better food and more of it, as improvements in agriculture and transport made food cheaper and more readily available. We should not imagine, however, that life was constantly improving for everyone. There were still many examples of families being short of food through low wages, unemployment, illness or old age.

Where did all the extra people live?

During the eighteenth century there was a major change in the pattern of population in Britain. Before the Industrial Revolution, the vast majority of people lived in the countryside and their lives revolved around farming. With the invention of an efficient steam engine and the growth of factories, people began to move into towns to work in the newly mechanised industries. It was during this period that many of our modern cities, such as Birmingham, Leeds and Manchester, the centre of the cotton industry, began to develop.

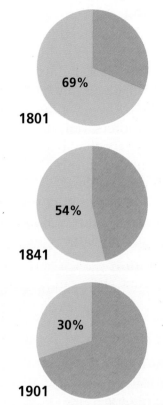

Percentage of population living in the countryside

69%
1801

54%
1841

30%
1901

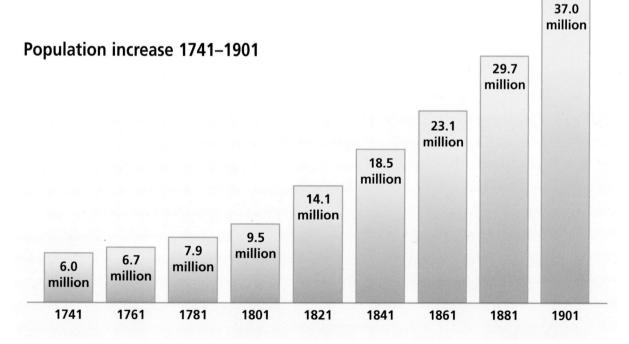

Population increase 1741–1901

6.0 million — 1741
6.7 million — 1761
7.9 million — 1781
9.5 million — 1801
14.1 million — 1821
18.5 million — 1841
23.1 million — 1861
29.7 million — 1881
37.0 million — 1901

Problems in the towns

The influx of people into the growing industrial towns produced a steady supply of workers for the new factories, but it also produced a number of problems.

Housing

As workers moved into towns, the factory owners built houses for them to live in. There were no planning regulations for the factory owners to follow, so they could build whatever kinds of house they wanted. Obviously, factory owners wanted to provide reasonable housing for their workers, but they did not want to spend more money than they had to. Buying land cost money, so it was important to build as many houses as possible on each piece of land. This meant that houses were built back-to-back in long rows. There were no gardens and very few windows. Rooms were small and since families were usually large, conditions were very cramped.

Sanitation

Very few workers' houses had running water, so people had to fetch their water from a pipe at the end of the street. There were also no toilets. It was not uncommon for whole streets to share one toilet. Can you imagine what it must have been like for 200–300 people to share one toilet? Of course, this toilet would not be an efficient flushing toilet like today. Instead the 'privy' would be a wooden seat over a hole called a 'cess pit'. From time to time, men were employed to empty the cess pits with buckets. But the job was so unpleasant that they were only allowed to work at night!

Source B

A description of the poorer area of Manchester in 1832:

Most of those districts in which the labouring poor live have houses which are ill-drained, often ill-ventilated and are unprovided with toilets. The streets, which are narrow, unpaved and worn into deep ruts, become the resting place of mud, refuse and disgusting rubbish.

In Parliament Street there is only one toilet for 380 inhabitants. It is placed in a narrow passage, from where there is a flow of muck which infests the close-by houses and must produce a fertile source of disease.

The city of Manchester in 1850.

Source C

Average age of death in 1840 in four English industrial towns. One of the reasons the ages are so low is because so many babies and children died before reaching adulthood.

	Labourers	Gentry
Bolton	18 years	34 years
Leeds	19 years	44 years
Liverpool	15 years	35 years
Manchester	17 years	38 years

A terraced street in London in 1872.

Source D

Things to do

1 Make a list of the reasons why conditions were so bad in Britain's cities in the nineteenth century.

2 a Using Sources B–F, explain how conditions in the mid-nineteenth century were different from life today.

   b Were there any bad things about the cities which still exist in our cities today?

3 Why did 'gentry' live longer than 'labourers' in Britain's cities in the nineteenth century?

4 If conditions in cities were so bad, why did so many people go to live there?

Source E

An account of the state of the River Aire, a main source of drinking water for the city of Leeds, written in 1841:

Into the river flow the contents of about 200 water closets [toilets] and similar places, a great number of common drains, the draining from dunghills, the Infirmary (dead leeches, poultices from patients, etc.), slaughter houses, chemical soap, gas, dung, dyehouses and factories, pig manure and all sorts of decomposed animal and vegetable substances.

This amounts to about 30 million gallons per year of filth flowing into the river between Armley Mills and the Kings Mill.

Source F

An extract from a report on the town of Greenock in 1844:

In one part of the town there is a dunghill with a hundred cubic yards of filth collected from all parts of the town. It belongs to a person who deals in dung; he sells it by the cartful. To please his customers he keeps it for some time before selling it. The heap is enclosed by a wall twelve feet high, but comes over the top of the wall. The filthy liquid oozes through the wall and runs over the pavement. There is a housing estate nearby and all food and drink must be covered; if it is left for a minute, the flies attack it and make it unfit for use, from the strong taste of the dunghill left by flies.

Cholera arrives!

In early 1830 word arrived in Britain of a new disease which had started in India and was sweeping across Europe. The disease was cholera. More than half of those who caught it died a very painful death. It was spread through water which had been contaminated by the faeces of those who already had the disease.

At that time people had little idea what caused cholera, but they soon found out how deadly it could be. The first case of the new disease occurred in Sunderland in late October 1831. The government ordered that the port of Sunderland should be closed but this did not stop the spread of the disease. Soon it was spreading across Britain and killed over 50,000 people. There were further outbreaks in 1848, 1854 and 1866.

Source G

A report in a local newspaper in Sunderland in early October 1831 – a few weeks before the outbreak of cholera in the town.

The following are the symptoms of the disease: giddiness, sick stomach, slow or weak pulse, cramp at the top of the fingers and toes. This is followed by vomiting and diarrhoea. The face becomes sharp and shrunken, the eyes sink and look wild, the lips, face, neck, hands and feet turn blue, purple, and black. The skin is deadly cold and often damp.

In the treatment of this disease no specific remedy has yet been discovered, nor has any cure been successful. But the greatest confidence can be expressed in the doctors of this country who will surely find a way to treat the disease.

How cholera spread from India to England.

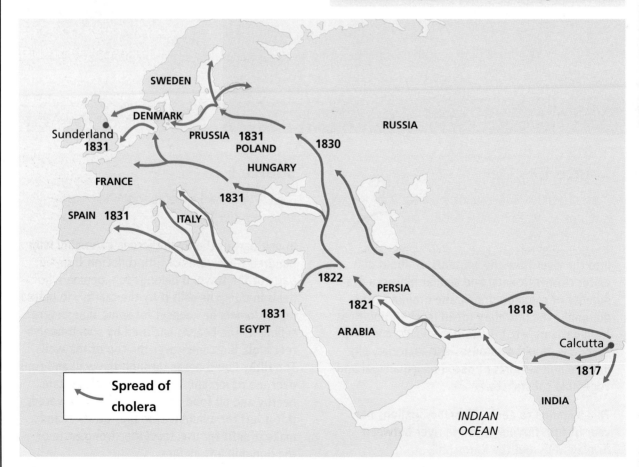

Source H

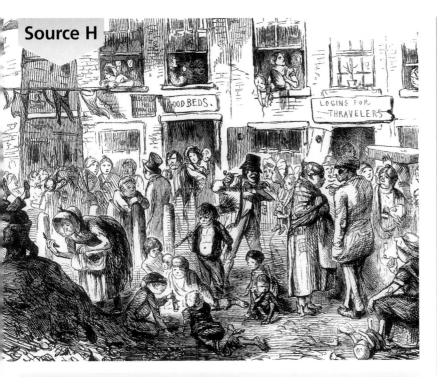

A Court for King Cholera – a cartoon from the time, showing the dreadful conditions in which some people lived.

Source I

An extract from a letter written to Lord Londonderry, by his doctor, J. Brown. Lord Londonderry was a Sunderland mine owner who could not export his coal from Sunderland because of government restrictions. On 13 November Lord Londonderry wrote to a London newspaper complaining about the restrictions and quoting Dr Brown.

My Lord,

After careful observation I have come to the following conclusions:

1 That cholera has not come to England from abroad.
2 That the disease is subsiding.
3 That the disease occurs most amongst the poor who live in the worst conditions and are already weak through previous diseases and too much alcohol.
4 The restrictions placed on trade are unnecessary because the disease is not infectious.

Your Lordship's Obedient Servant,

Dr J. Brown

Things to do

1 Draw a diagram of a human body and label it to show:
   a the symptoms of cholera
   b how it was spread.

2 People in England must have known that cholera was coming their way for some years. So why didn't they do something to stop it spreading?

3 Do you think the report in the Sunderland newspaper (Source G) was written just because people would find it interesting? Could there be another reason?

4 How much of what is written in Source I do you believe? Explain how you decided on your answer.

Source J

Part of the report into conditions in Leeds published in the *Sanitary Conditions of the Labouring Population of Great Britain* in 1842:

By the inspection of the map which has been prepared at my request to show where the disease has broken out, I can see that it is most common in the uncleansed and close streets occupied by the labouring poor. In the badly cleansed and badly drained areas the number of deaths is almost twice that of the areas with better conditions.

Dark, satanic mills?

The invention of a reliable form of power (steam) and the development of impressive new machinery meant that the Domestic System gradually died out and was replaced by the Factory System. From now on, industrial workers would come to the factory instead of working from home.

One of the first industries affected by this change was textile manufacture. Early inventors such as Richard Arkwright had developed machines which were too big to be used in the home and so were set up in factories using water for power. One such factory was the famous Cromford Mill in Derbyshire. However, later inventions, such as Cartwright's Power Loom, needed steam to be effective. By the early years of the nineteenth century, both cotton and wool manufacture were becoming dominated by factories using steam for power.

Working conditions

The purpose of the factories was to make money. This was done by working employees for as long as possible and paying low wages. Inside the factories, conditions were poor. Cotton manufacture required high temperatures to prevent the thread snapping and, of course, the steam engines also made factories hot. Dangerous machinery was not fenced off and there were no safety regulations.

Source K

TO
Journeymen Spinner

Wanted Immediately,
From Eighty to One Hundre
MULE SPINNERS,

For a New Mill and other Mills, in Great Bolton, which New Mill is complete with new Machinery now ready gaite and will commence running on Monday Morning next, a joining to which Mills are a Number of Cottages, for th convenience and accommodation of Spinners: liberal Wag will be given and constant employ.

For further particulars apply to Messrs. ORMROD an HARDCASTLE, of Bolton aforesaid, Cotton Spinners.

An advertisement for spinners to work in a new mill in Bolton in 1816.

Source M

A picture of children working in a textile factory. This picture comes from a novel written in 1840, giving an account of the sad life of an orphan boy.

Source L

A selection of fines for workers at a cotton mill near Manchester in 1823.

Having a window open	1 shilling
Whistling	1 shilling
Dirty at work	1 shilling
Being five minutes late	1 shilling
Being sick and not sending a replacement	6 shillings

Laws to improve working conditions

Factory Act 1819: Children to work no more than 12 hours a day

Factory Act 1833: Children under 9 not to work in textile mills. 10–13-year-olds limited to 48 hours' work a week

Factory Act 1844: Women limited to 12 hours' work a day

Factory Act 1847: Women and children limited to 10 hours' work a day

Factory Act 1850: Women and children's work limit increased to 10.5 hours but must be between 6 a.m. and 6 p.m.

Factory Act 1874: No worker to work more than 56.5 hours per week

Things to do

1 Look at Source K. What could a historian learn about the Factory System from this source?

2 Some of the fines in Source L seem to be for rather strange reasons. Can you explain why these were chosen as offences to be punished?

3 Do you think that Source M gives a true picture of life inside a textile factory?

4 Why do you think factory owners liked employing women and children?

5 Write a short speech either:
   a criticising working conditions in factories, or
   b explaining why they were not really so bad.

Punishments were very harsh in the factories. Fines were common and 'overseers' were employed to check that work was being done properly. If not, corporal punishment was often used to encourage better work. Children were employed in the factories from a very early age and often had the job of 'scavenging' under the machines to pick up waste cotton or wool. The use of machines meant that women and children could do most of the work, since little muscle power was needed.

Cruel?

There have been criticisms of the conditions in factories and most employers have been portrayed as cruel. However, we must consider things from the perspective of people at the time. Workers coming into factories from agricultural work were used to working very long hours in difficult conditions. They were also used to their children working. In many families the children's wages were vital to life. But agricultural workers were not used to working to the clock. Five minutes late meant nothing in a field, but cost the employer money in wasted steam in a factory. To train workers to be punctual, employers sometimes had to use harsh punishments.

Some factory owners, such as Robert Owen, treated their workers better than most owners did. There were also large numbers of **reformers** who campaigned for change and helped get laws passed to improve conditions. But we must be careful not to let factory owners off too lightly!

Source N

An account of a day in the life of a mill girl, written by William Dodd, a factory reformer, in 1842.

Too poor to own a clock, her family pays a watchman to tap on the window at 4.30 each morning. After she drinks coffee and eats bread, the mill bell warns her to hurry. At 5.30 work begins. Two hours later the pace of the machines slackens enough to allow her to clean off the dust and have breakfast – if she is quick. At noon the machines stop and she cleans them thoroughly before rushing home for soup and bread. She is back in place by one o'clock and works until seven. After cleaning her machines again, she returns home fourteen hours after setting off. This is six days a week (though she may get home early on a Sunday).

Source A

Registration District	City of London

1842. Marriage solemnized at 106 Shoe Lane
in the — of West London in the City of London

No.	When married	Name and surname	Age	Condition	Rank or profession	Residence at the time of marriage	Father's name and surname	Rank or profession of father
1	September 28th	George Woolf	full	Bachelor	Accountant	106 Shoe Lane	Joseph Woolf	—
		Maria Mordecai	—	Spinster	—	20 John Street Waterloo Road	Jonas Mordecai	

Married in the Congregation of the New Synagogue according to the Rites & Ceremonies of the German & Polish Jews by me Abm Baslett Reader

This marriage was solemnized between us, George Woolf / Maria Woolf   In the presence of us, P. Harris / Moses Levy   J. L. Lindenthal Registrar

A detail from the marriage certificate of George Woolf and Maria Mordecai, September 1842.

Maria Mordecai and George Woolf were married on 28 September 1842 in George's home, 106 Shoe Lane, London. Maria and George were Jews whose families had fled from persecution in central Europe in the eighteenth century. The wedding was attended by George's brothers and sisters, Sophia, Hannah, Julia, Elizabeth, Fanny, Samuel and Philip, together with his father, Joseph, and mother, Alcry. We know that Maria's father, Jonas, was also present but we do not know which other relatives were there.

Cholera

On 18 April 1844 Maria gave birth to a son, who was named Joseph after his grandfather. In 1849 Maria became pregnant once more. But in June disaster struck the Woolf family. Cholera! Their home in Shoe Lane was in a row of tall, dark houses which rarely saw sunlight. The inhabitants drew their water from the nearby Fleet Brook. This was the same brook into which household waste from the streets would have gone. It was a perfect breeding ground for cholera.

Source B

This drawing of George Woolf was made in 1858 from an earlier lost portrait.

Source C

Joseph Woolf, the son of George and Maria, drawn in 1858.

Source D

No.	When and where died	Name and surname	Sex	Age	Occupation	Cause of death	Signature, description, and residence of informant	When registered	Signature of registrar

REGISTRATION DISTRICT _West London_

_1849._ DEATH in the Sub-district of _West London_ in the _City of London_

Columns :— 1, 2, 3, 4, 5, 6, 7, 8, 9

| 100 | Eighteenth June 1849 106 Shoe Lane St. Brides | Maria Woolf | Female | 32 years. | Wife of George Woolf Accountant. | Diarrhoea 8 days Cholera 4 days Premature Labour 32 hours Exhaustion Certified. | G. Woolf Present at the Death 106 Shoe Lane London. | Nineteenth June 1849 | William Nason Registrar |

A detail from the death certificate of Maria Woolf, June 1849.

Death

A cholera epidemic hit Britain in 1848–9 and 62,000 people died. No one knew how it spread. Maria, seven months pregnant, caught the disease. The people with her would have tried desperately to keep her cool by sponging her down and giving her water to drink. The water, however, would have come from the Fleet Brook. Within eight days both Maria and her premature baby were dead.

George and his son Joseph survived the cholera epidemic. George died two years later from tuberculosis. Joseph was brought up by his Aunt Julia and Uncle Joel. He died in 1911 having worked all his life as a furniture upholsterer.

Source F

Kate Vaughan-Williams, a modern doctor, said this about Maria Woolf's death.

Maria probably had cholera for eight days, from when the diarrhoea first started. She would have had acute pain in her abdomen; smelly, explosive, watery diarrhoea and a high fever. All this would have triggered off early labour. A long labour like that would increase risk of infection. She was probably bleeding heavily, too. Eventually her circulatory system would have collapsed and then she died.

Source E

A mourning ring, made after Maria Woolf's death. It contains woven strands of Maria's hair. The ring would have been worn by her husband, or another relative, in memory of Maria.

Things to do

You have been asked to prepare a report on Maria Woolf and her family using the evidence on these pages. Here is how you do it:

1 Look carefully at the marriage certificate and Maria's death certificate. What information can you get from these documents?

2 a Use the information in the text to draw up a family tree for George and Maria.
  b The family tree has some gaps in it. Do you know how a historian could fill in those gaps?

3 Make a list of all the facts that you can find about Maria and her family in the text and sources on these pages.

4 Now write your report on 'Maria Woolf and her family'.

Source A

Bradford in the 1840s.

The first factory, a wool spinning mill, was built in 1803. By 1840 over thirty more spinning mills had been built and the population had grown from around 13,000 to about 67,000. Bradford mills specialised in making worsted.

Woolcombing at home

Woolcombing was a filthy job. In Bradford the woolcombers worked where they lived – in the slum houses and courtyards surrounding the spinning mills. Often whole families lived in just one room. This was usually the room where the men worked all day at woolcombing. The women and children were working in the local mill, using machinery to spin thread from the wool the men had hand-combed.

The process of woolcombing

The combers worked with raw wool – the oily fleeces straight from the sheep shearers. Their job was to comb the wool so that only the long, straight fibres were left to be spun into thread at the mill. First the combers stoked charcoal stoves until they were hot enough to heat up the metal combs. These were heavy and T-shaped with up to 120 long steel teeth. When the combs were hot enough, the combers fastened one comb to a wooden post and threw a large handful of oily wool onto the hot teeth. Then the combers pulled another hot comb through the wool, unravelling the fibres and laying them straight.

Worsted

To make worsted the raw wool is first combed to separate out the long fibres from the short. The long fibres are then spun to make a strong, supple thread which, when woven, makes a light, smooth fabric.

Woollen cloth

To make woollen cloth the wool is first **carded** so that all the fibres run in the same direction. All the fibres, long and short, are spun into thread which, when woven, makes a dense, solid fabric.

Only one room

This went on until all the fleeces had been combed. The air in the room would be thick with fumes from the charcoal stoves and the stench of oily wool. In the evening the stoves were dampened down and work stopped. The women and children returned from the mill and the room was needed for cooking, eating and sleeping.

Fighting for a fair wage

By the 1820s the woolcombers were becoming discontented. The mill owners were making large profits from worsted manufacturing and the combers felt their wages should be increased. They formed a union, but the mill owners refused to take any notice of it. In 1825 the woolcombers went on strike. It got them nowhere. The owners steadily reduced their wages until, by 1837, woolcombers were earning half the wage of 1825.

Machinery – the final threat

The woolcombers were to face a far bigger threat than harsh mill owners. For some years Samuel Lister had been trying to develop a machine that would comb wool. In 1843 he produced the first sample of machine-combed wool. His machine cost £200 to make – and sold for £1200. Mill owners snapped them up and by the 1850s Samuel Lister was a very rich man. But thousands of woolcombers were thrown out of work. Some re-trained to work on the new machines; many more tried to find other work. But such large-scale unemployment made their situation desperate. Thousands faced starvation.

In 1848, £2000 was allocated by the Council from Bradford city rates to help those woolcombers who wanted to emigrate.

By 1858 no hand-woolcombers were working anywhere in the worsted industry.

Source B

An advertisement written by the Woolcombers' Aid Association in 1848.

Wanted: Situations as Passenger or Goods Porters for 100 Strong, Active, Honest and Industrious Woolcombers from 22 to 40 years of age, varying in height from 5ft 6in to 6ft.

Source C

Part of the report of the Bradford Sanatory Committee on living conditions in Bradford, 1845. Woolcombers lived in the places described here.

Pinfold Street: The back part of the street has filthy yards and cellars in which the inmates are crowded together. The fumes of charcoal breed diseases. Children died of fever here in the last few weeks and women are suffering from various illnesses.

Back Adelaide Street: Very damp – no ventilation – privy [toilet] ten feet three inches from the door – three persons work and sleep in this dirty and confined cellar, five feet three inches below the surface.

Mary Gate: Upper apartment contains three charcoal stoves at which six persons work – there are two beds in the same room in which four persons sleep – bad smell – very hot.

Nelson Court: There are a number of cellars in it utterly unfit for human dwellings. No drainage whatever. The visitors [people writing the report] cannot find words to express their horror of the filth, stench and misery, and were unable to bear the overpowering stench which comes from a common sewer.

Things to do

1 Life for most workers in industrial Britain was hard. What clues can you find here that a woolcomber's life was particularly hard?

2 Design a poster which could have been used by the Woolcombers' Aid Association to ask for help for the woolcombers.

3 Use all the information in this unit to write a story or a poem about a woolcomber in Bradford who lost his job because of the coming of machinery. You could think about whether he was, for example, pleased that a dreadful way of life was over, or sad and anxious because he would have to look for work elsewhere; perhaps he blamed – or thanked – the factory owners; perhaps he blamed – or thanked – the machinery itself.

A grand funeral

On 6 January 1877 the city of Bradford came to a halt. No smoke belched from the hundreds of factory chimneys; flags flew at half-mast; 100,000 people lined the streets and all police leave was stopped. Four horses with black plumes on their heads pulled a **hearse** from Halifax, through Bradford to Saltaire. Seventy carriages followed, carrying the mourners. These were family mourners and anyone of any importance in the industrial north: mill owners and magistrates, MPs and clergymen, peers and chief constables. This was the funeral procession of Titus Salt, one of the most respected mill owners in Yorkshire.

Bradford in the 1830s

In 1834, when he was thirty-one years old, Titus Salt set up his first worsted mill and started to make his fortune. What was Bradford like in the 1830s? It was in the middle of a tremendous upheaval. In 1800 it was a collection of small weaving villages. By 1850 it had 129 factories and a population of over 100,000. Cheap houses were hastily built; roads and sewers couldn't cope. There was terrible overcrowding, dirt and disease in the poorer areas, with clouds of pollution hanging over the whole town.

Making a fortune

By the mid-1840s Titus Salt had made a fortune. This was partly because of **mechanisation**. One by one the processes which converted wool into worsted cloth were taken over by machines. Salt's mills were equipped with spinning machines, then weaving machines and, finally, with combing machines. All this meant that worsted could be produced cheaply – and that it sold well and quickly.

The mystery ingredient

In 1836 Titus Salt made a business trip to Liverpool. There he saw some 300 bales of something called 'Peruvian wool' which no one wanted.

Source A

Titus Salt (1803–76) did not like publicity. This is a rare photograph of him.

Source B

From *Titus Salt and Saltaire* written by John Styles in 1990:

The two waterways that ran through the town – Bradford Beck and the Bradford Canal – were open sewers. In the 1840s the canal was known as 'River Stink'. Smoke poured from factory chimneys, irritating throat and lungs and soiling clothes and buildings.

Average expectation of life in the town in the 1840s was barely twenty years, the lowest in Yorkshire. The rate of infant mortality was the fifth highest in the country.

Popular discontent was shown at meetings and rallies, demonstrations and riots. Bradford was a town where tens of thousands of people took to the streets to demand limits on hours of work in factories, official help for unemployed hand-loom weavers and woolcombers, and the repeal of the hated New Poor Law.

These dresses, the height of fashion in 1862, were made from alpaca. Queen Victoria had several dresses made from alpaca which was specially spun and woven for her in Titus Salt's mills.

Alpaca

Titus took some of this 'wool' home to show his father, who told him not to buy it under any circumstances. Titus bought the whole consignment. With trusted assistants he worked for eighteen months perfecting a way of spinning it into thread. The 'Peruvian wool' was alpaca from Peruvian goats and was to make Titus Salt extremely rich. Titus and his team perfected a way of weaving alpaca with cotton and silk to make a light, slightly shiny cloth which could easily be made up into fashionable women's clothes.

Cornering the market

Titus Salt did not want anyone copying this worsted. It wasn't always easy to get regular supplies from South America. So Salt and two other trusted manufacturers bought up all the supplies of alpaca as soon as they arrived in England. This made sure Salt could keep making this expensive cloth, which rich people would always be able to afford.

A good master

Titus Salt paid good wages and did not lay his workers off when times were bad. This was because his luxury cloth made huge profits. People wanted to work for him, and his workforce was hardworking and loyal. But he was to do more for his workers than this. He moved them out of filthy, polluted Bradford into the purpose-built village of Saltaire.

Source D

From *Salt and Silver* written in 1997 by Jim Greenhalf.

In 1834, when Salt set up in business, alpaca imports amounted to a mere 5,700 lbs. Six years later that had grown to an avalanche: 1,325,000 lbs, most of it arriving in the West Riding [of Yorkshire] by canal barge and cart. For about a quarter of a century from 1840, bright alpaca mixed fabrics took the world by storm.

Things to do

1 What were the two main ways in which Titus Salt made his fortune?

2 a Describe Titus Salt's funeral.
   b Would the funeral of an important person today be the same or different?

3 Read about Bradford in the 1830s.
   a Which words would you use to describe the town: dangerous; exciting; frightening; prosperous?

b Would someone living at the time have used the same words?
Explain your answer, using evidence from this unit to back up what you say.

4 What clues can you get from this unit as to why Titus Salt decided to move his factory and his workers out of Bradford?

Salt's Mill

The mill was the first building to be put up at Saltaire. It was enormous – larger than any mill in Bradford – and had, under one roof, absolutely everything needed to turn wool, cotton, silk and alpaca into a beautiful, glowing and expensive cloth. It was officially opened on 20 September 1853, which was Titus Salt's fiftieth birthday. He held a huge party for 3500 mill workers in the new combing shed. But these mill workers had to travel the three miles from Bradford each day to work in the Saltaire mill and so Titus Salt began to build a village for them on the other side of the railway line from the mill.

Houses

Salt believed that good housing produced good workers. His houses were well built; every one had a yard and an outside lavatory which was emptied regularly. They were carefully graded, according to the occupation of the tenant, and the rent varied according to the size of the house. Workmen's houses had a living room, kitchen and, upstairs, two bedrooms. The houses of overlookers (supervisors) had a **scullery**, kitchen, living room, three bedrooms and a front garden. Managers, designers and wool buyers had the best houses. The streets were named after members of Salt's family, like Albert Road, Ada Street and George Street. By 1871 Titus Salt had built 824 houses in which 4–5000 of his workers lived.

Spare time

Saltaire had churches, almshouses for the elderly, a school and a hospital. But Titus Salt also worried about what his workers would do in their spare time. Spare time, to Salt and other mill owners, meant workers might get drunk, idle or violent.

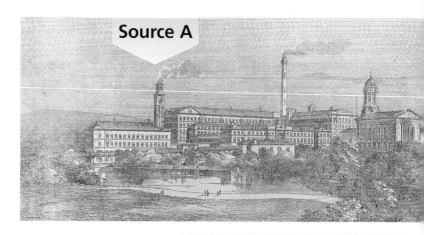

Source A

Salt's Mill, the first building in Saltaire. This etching was made in 1885.

Source B

These are modern photographs of houses in Saltaire. The top picture of Ada Street were workmen's houses and those in George Street, below, were for overlookers.

Source C

Roberts Park, Saltaire, in 1874. The park covered 14 acres of landscaped ground close to the mill and the church. All sorts of activities were available: swimming, archery, boating, bowls and cricket. There were strict rules: gambling, swearing, stone throwing and drunkenness were forbidden. Dogs were not allowed in the park, neither were children under eight except with an adult.

They would also have time to get hold of **Chartist** and **socialist** ideas, and – possibly worst of all – young people would have time for sex. Titus Salt was determined to give his workers suitable ways of spending their leisure time.

He refused to allow any pubs in Saltaire. Instead he gave money to support all sorts of different societies: a cricket club, a fishing club and a gardening society. But more important than the clubs was the Institute. This building held a concert hall, lecture theatre, library, school of art and classrooms. There was also a reading room, chess and draughts room, smoking room, billiards room and gym. It was here that Titus Salt expected his workers to spend most of their spare time. And it was a success. Membership was cheap and the Institute quickly had over a thousand members.

A gentle prison?

Titus Salt was both an employer and a landlord, so he had enormous power over his employees. Workers who were dismissed had to leave the village, so they lost their house and friends as well as their job. Strikes just didn't happen in Saltaire and even trade disputes were rare. It is important to remember that people who went to work for Salt knew what Saltaire was like and knew the sort of standards of behaviour that were expected of them. Many Bradford mill workers sneered and jeered at Salt's workers for being so obedient. However, there were always plenty of people wanting work in Salt's Mill. Saltaire gave mill workers, who were prepared to obey the rules, the chance to live in better surroundings.

Things to do

1 Titus Salt made a fortune by spinning and weaving alpaca in Bradford. He did not have to create Saltaire. Why do you think he did so? Can you find any clues in this unit and the one before it?

2 Make a list of the advantages and disadvantages, to a mill worker, of living in Saltaire and working in Salt's Mill.

3 With the person next to you, write, and then act out, a conversation between Mary, who works in Bradford mill, and Ann, who works for Salt and lives in Saltaire. They are comparing their living conditions.
You could start like this:
Mary: Why on earth are you working for Salt? You can't live your own life.
Ann: But I have a dry, comfortable house which is a lot better than your damp two rooms.
Mary: That's not everything – what about the things you can't do? Salt rules your life!

4 Would you agree that Saltaire was a 'gentle prison'?

Early in 1783 a wealthy young man was touring Lancashire on horseback. He seemed particularly interested in rivers and whether they were running swiftly or slowly. What was he doing? He was neither having a holiday nor planning a crime. He was looking for somewhere to build a factory.

Who was Samuel Greg?

Samuel Greg was a very successful textile merchant based in Manchester. The 1780s were exciting times for men like Samuel with money to spend. There were fortunes to be made by people with vision who were willing to take a risk. This was because inventors like James Hargreaves, Richard Arkwright and Samuel Crompton had developed machinery that spun raw cotton quickly and efficiently into thread. Was it worth investing in this new machinery? Samuel thought it was, and decided to take the risk and build a cotton-spinning mill.

Finding a site

Samuel Greg eventually found what he was looking for: a source of power in a valley where it would be possible to build a spinning mill. Ten miles south of Manchester, close to the village of Styal, the river Bollin cut through a sandstone valley. This river, so Samuel believed, was fast-running enough to be able to turn a water wheel and power the spinning mill he was going to build. He checked his figures, and then, in 1784, rented the land and the rights over the water from the Earl of Stamford and Warrington who owned them. Samuel had taken the first steps to becoming a cotton mill owner and the head of a vast business empire.

An eighteenth-century map of the area around Styal.

Source A

Samuel Greg as a young man.

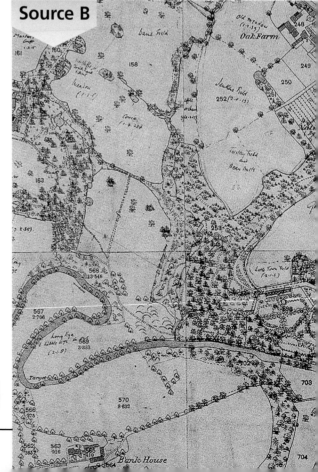

Source B

Finding workers

Samuel Greg had nearly everything he needed for a successful operation: money to build a mill and power to drive the new machinery. But he needed something else: people to work the new machinery. Styal was a small, isolated village. Many people living there worked on the land. Some did a little spinning at home and finished mohair buttons for Macclesfield manufacturers. None of them would ever have worked in a factory and few of them would even have seen one. This doesn't seem to have bothered Samuel Greg. He spent £16,000 building and equipping Quarry Bank Mill and after six years 183 adults and children were working there.

Where had Samuel Greg found his workers? Some were local people. Some came from his works at Eyam in Derbyshire and he may have poached some from other mill owners. However, until the 1840s more than half of his workers were children who came from local workhouses. Greg built a large Apprentice House close to the mill for them, and cottages in Styal village for his adult workers.

A successful enterprise?

Samuel Greg was an **entrepreneur**. He had the money and vision, and was willing to take risks. But he did not have the technical knowledge needed to develop cotton spinning in ways that would bring him most profit. He went into partnership, first with John Massey and then with Peter Ewart. Together they extended the mill buildings to house more machinery, improved the water courses and put in a second water wheel. By the end of the century Samuel Greg was a prosperous mill owner. His gamble had paid off.

Source C

A modern photograph of the front of Quarry Bank Mill, showing the old mill built by Samuel Greg (1784–96) and part of the new mill.

Why build a mill at Styal?

- Cash was available.
- Power was available from the river Bollin.
- New machinery had been invented.
- Wages for mill workers were low.
- 1783: the ending of the American War of Independence opened up new markets for cotton goods.
- 1780s: mill owners no longer had to pay for a licence to use the new inventions.

Things to do

1 What three things were needed before anyone would be likely to finance a new mill?

2 Read **Why build a mill at Styal?** above. Samuel Greg must have thought about all these points.
   a List them in what you think would have been his order of importance.
   b Should he have taken anything else into consideration before coming to a decision?

Many jobs in cotton mills could be done by children, such as cleaning under moving machinery or piecing together snapped threads. Children were paid less than adults and were easier to train and discipline. At the time of the first cotton mills, parish authorities were having to deal with large numbers of pauper children. Hundreds of these children were sent to work in cotton mills. Quarry Bank Mill got its children first from the workhouse at Newcastle-under-Lyme and then from the Liverpool workhouse. Around 100 children were sent from Liverpool to Quarry Bank Mill in the 1820s and 1830s. Esther Price was one of these children.

Source A

A girl scavenging under a spinning mule. Mules like this were operating in Quarry Bank Mill when Esther Price was there.

From workhouse to Apprentice House

Esther was born in Liverpool on 8 March 1820. She had two brothers, Richard and John, and two sisters, Margaret and Martha. We don't know why, or when, Esther was sent to the workhouse. We don't know whether she went alone or with her whole family. We do know that on 3 May 1831, when Esther was eleven years old, she was at Quarry Bank Mill being examined by the mill's doctor.

Esther Price's baptismal certificate. This was given to her parents when they took her to church to be baptised.

Samuel Greg would not take weak or sick children. At first, Esther was said to be 'delicate'. The mill's doctor thought she was nine years old, not eleven. However, she must have got stronger because, at the end of 1833, she was legally **apprenticed** to Samuel Greg. Again, there was a muddle about her age. The **indenture** said she was twelve when she was really thirteen years old.

Source B

BAPTISMS solemnized in the Parish Church of ST. PETER, LIVERPOOL, in the Year One Thousand Eight Hundred and *Twenty*

When Baptized.	Child's Christian Name.	Parents' Name. Christian	Surname.	Abode.	Quality, Trade, or Profession	By whom the Ceremony was performed.
1820 May 23. No. 49	Esther	Thomas & Maria	Price	Harrison Street	Awl Maker	P. Bulmer Curate

The above is a true Copy, taken from the Register of Baptisms in the Parish Church of ST. PETER, in LIVERPOOL, this *Twenty Eighth* Day of *October* in the Year One Thousand Eight Hundred and Thirty *Six*

Born March 8th 1820. Reg. Book St Peter's

By me *Wm Maybrick*

PARISH CLERK

A modern photograph of the Apprentice House at Quarry Bank Mill. Esther Price lived here 1833–8.

A troublesome girl

In August 1835 Mr and Mrs Timperley took over the running of the Apprentice House. Very soon the place was in uproar. In November Esther and another girl assaulted an apprentice so badly that they were sent to the local magistrates' court. Two other girls were given a week's solitary confinement in the Apprentice House for disorderly behaviour.

Running away

In August 1836 Esther ran away with her friend Lucy Garner. Lucy went back after five days but Esther stayed away for ten. A pamphlet written at the time says that Esther had gone to Liverpool to see her father while there was no work at the mill. She had asked permission but had been refused. So she took off after work on Saturday and returned at breakfast time on the Wednesday. The mill stopped working on the Monday and Tuesday. Other girls were given permission to visit their parents for quite long periods, but Esther was not.

Punishment

Both girls were put in solitary confinement, Lucy for three days and Esther for a week. Esther was kept in a room in the Apprentice House. The windows were boarded up so that she could neither talk to the others nor escape. She had to sleep on the floor. Every morning and evening she was given milk, bread and porridge to eat. After four days, Mrs Timperley died unexpectedly. Esther, afraid of being left alone with a dead body in the house, begged to be released. She was let out two days early.

Happy endings?

In January 1837 Esther met her sister in the Horseshoe pub. She gave Esther her baptismal certificate. Esther used her baptismal certificate to prove her age and so end her apprenticeship. When her apprenticeship ended, Esther stayed on at the mill for the rest of her working life. Esther's problems were used by supporters of the Ten Hours' Movement, which campaigned for a reduction in the working hours of women and children.

Things to do

1 **a** Why did Samuel Greg employ children?
   b What were the advantages and disadvantages of employing children from workhouses?

2 What information about Esther can you get from Source B?

3 Why do you think the mill was muddled about Esther's age?

4 **a** Why do you think Esther ran away?
   b Why do you think she was treated so harshly on her return?

Disaster in the pit

As the demand for coal grew during the Industrial Revolution, thousands of small 'pit villages' sprang up in the main coalfields of Britain. One area where this was particularly true was north-east England. In the Northumberland and Durham coalfields there were hundreds of pits and many of them were surrounded by small villages, which existed simply because the pit was there.

In such villages the whole population depended upon the pit. Those who were not working there had jobs which supplied miners and their families with their food and clothing or helped run the service industries that kept a village alive. Everyone had friends or relatives that worked in the pit and everyone lived in fear that one of the regular disasters that occurred in the mining industry would happen to their pit.

On 25 May 1812 the people of Felling felt the ground shake under their feet. They knew their worst fears were about to come true.

Source D

An extract from the list of those killed at Felling Colliery, 25 May 1812:

Name	Job	Age
Thomas Craggs	Hewer	36
Thomas Craggs	Trapper	9
John Greener	Hewer	21
Edward Richardson	Hewer	39
Robert Dobson	Trapper	13
William Dixon	Hewer	35
George Robson	Putter	15
Andrew Allan	Trapper	11
John Thompson	Hewer	36
John Pearson	Hewer	64
Thomas Bears	Hewer	48
Charles Wilson	Hewer	48
Joseph Gordon	Trapper	10
Robert Gordon	Hewer	40
Thomas Gordon	Trapper	8

Explosion at Felling pit!

The pit at Felling began work in May 1811. The best methods of ventilation known at the time were used, but in spite of this the pit exploded on 25 May 1812.

The deep places where the explosions took place restricted the force so that the full noise was not heard on the surface. For half a mile the trembling of the ground was the first sign of the explosion and then for four miles the noise of hollow rumblings in the air was heard. Immense quantities of coal, pieces of wood and dust drove high in the air and some bodies of injured men were thrown up the shaft.

The scene was dreadful, in all directions roads and paths were covered with coal dust and bits of machinery and the area was enveloped in darkness. The explosion had wrecked all the machinery and it was not until fresh machinery could be brought that steps could be taken to see what had happened. When this was done only 32 out of the 120 men and boys employed in the mine were rescued alive. Three of these died afterwards, suffering from burns and injuries.

After the blast some fearless men descended into the pit to see what had happened, but after a few attempts they had to return to the surface without being able to tell those waiting what had happened to their menfolk and children. The pit owners decided to put the fire out by sealing the pit and depriving it of oxygen.

The pit was not re-opened until 7 July 1812, when a great cloud of smoke came out of the shaft. Despite the time the pit had been closed, a great crowd of people assembled at the pit head hoping that their relatives might still be alive. When men descended into the pit they saw a horrific sight. Masses of rock had been hurled in every direction, wagons shattered and twisted, bodies of men, so mutilated that they could not be recognised.

From a report of the Felling Pit Disaster written shortly after the explosion.

Source E

Deaths in pits in the North-East 1793–1813.

This list was produced in the nineteenth century and the compiler wrote: 'Note this list is necessarily incomplete because of the lack of records.'

Date		Pit	Deaths
27 Dec	1793	Sheriff Hall, Gateshead	14
9 June	1794	Picton	30
11 June	1794	Harraton, Chester-le-Street	28
24 April	1795	Benwell, Newcastle	11
11 Oct	1799	Lumley	39
25 Sept	1803	Wallsend	13
21 Oct	1805	Hepburn, Newcastle	35
29 Nov	1805	Oxclose	38
28 March	1806	Killingworth	10
14 Sept	1809	Killingworth	12
25 May	1812	Felling	92
10 Oct	1812	Herrington	24
28 Sept	1813	Fatfield	32
24 Dec	1813	Felling	22

Source F

A trapper at work underground. This picture was produced in a government report on the employment of children in 1842.

Jobs done in the mine

Trapper: A child who opened and closed ventilation doors underground.

Hewer: A miner who cut the coal underground using a pick axe.

Putter: A miner (usually a young man) who pushed the coal tubs between the coal face and the shaft bottom.

Source G

These words were found scratched onto a water bottle belonging to Michael Smith. He was one of 164 miners who died after being trapped underground in an explosion at Seaham Colliery in County Durham in 1880.

Dear Margaret

There were forty of us all together at 7 a.m. Some were singing hymns, but my thoughts were on my little Michael, that he and I would meet in heaven at some time. Oh dear wife, God save you and the children and pray for me. Dear wife farewell, my last thoughts are about you and the children. Be sure and learn the children to pray for me. Oh what an awful position we are in.

Things to do

1 What use could a historian make of the information given in Source D?

2 a According to Source E, how many different disasters were there in the pits of north-east England from 1793 to 1813?

 b How many people were killed in total?

 c How many years are covered in the table in Source E? (Take care!)

 d How many people were killed on average each year?

 e How reliable do you think these figures are?

3 a Why might people have been surprised that there was an explosion at Felling Pit in May 1812?

 b What was the scene like after the accident?

 c How was the fire underground eventually put out?

 d The pit was not re-opened until 7 July 1812.

 i Was there any chance of people still being alive?

 ii Why do you think so many people assembled at the pit head?

4 What does the information on pages 58– 61 tell you about:

 a children in the mines

 b life in pit villages?

Roads

Most roads in the eighteenth century were muddy tracks linking village to village and villages to market towns. Pack horses and large wagons carried goods; business men travelled by horseback. Most other people walked. But change was on the way.

Turnpike Trusts

Turnpike Trusts were groups of people who got together to keep a stretch of road in good repair. They put gates and toll-houses at each end and charged travellers for using the road. Turnpikes employed specialist road builders, like Thomas Telford (1757–1834) and John McAdam (1756–1836). The roads they built meant that long distance travellers could use wheeled coaches. By about 1800 all of the larger towns in Britain were connected by turnpike roads.

Stagecoaches and mail coaches

Stagecoaches made their journeys in regular stages; hence the name. While stable-lads changed the horses, passengers would have a quick meal at the inn before setting off again. In 1784 the Post Office started running mail coaches and by 1792 there were 150 specially built coaches on the road. They carried passengers as well, but they had a rough ride until 1805 when Obadiah Elliott invented metal coach springs! Goods carriers copied the stagecoaches by running a timetabled service, and they, like the mail coach operators, allowed passengers to sit amongst the parcels.

Source A

This painting from 1839 shows a stagecoach passing through a turnpike at night.

Source B

William Cobbett, writing in 1818, describes the scene at a coaching inn:

The beautiful horses, impatient to be off. The inside of the coach full and the outside covered with men, women and children, boxes, bags and bundles. The coachman taking his reins in one hand and the whip in the other gives a signal with his foot and away they go at a speed of seven miles per hour. One of these coaches coming in, after a long journey, is a fascinating sight. The horses are all sweat and foam. Everything is covered with dust and dirt. But it still comes in, as regular as the hands of a clock.

Source C

Turnpiked and unturnpiked roads in 1838.

**Turnpiked road = 21,735 miles
Typical journey time = 7 miles per hour**

**Unturnpiked road = 103,707 miles
Typical journey time = 3 miles per hour**

Canals

Road improvements helped people to move around the country, but it was difficult and expensive to transport heavy goods in that way. Rivers and the sea were used to transport goods like coal and iron, but not every merchant worked close to the coast or to a navigable river. Canals were the answer. These were man-made waterways used to join up existing rivers. The very first canal was the Sankey Cut. It opened in 1757 for barges to carry Lancashire coal to Liverpool. Four years later the Duke of Bridgewater paid for a canal to carry coal from his mine at Worsley to Manchester. From then on, canals were paid for by groups of investors.

Canal mania

Canals were expensive to build. The men who invested money in them hoped to be rich. In the 1790s there was a mad rush to invest in canals. Many silly and impractical schemes were dreamed up and a lot of people lost a lot of money. But the good schemes worked. The Leeds to Liverpool canal, for example, was finished in 1816 and was a great success. As well as carrying heavy raw materials, canals were also good at transporting delicate, breakable goods. Josiah Wedgwood, whose company made fine china, invested in canals and used them because they transported his product smoothly.

The most important canals in Britain in about 1830. Canals linked almost all of England to the four major ports of London, Bristol, Liverpool and Hull.

Source D

An advertisement for canal transport in the *Birmingham Gazette*, 1811.

Thomas Coleman loads daily for Liverpool, Manchester and Chester. From Liverpool goods can be shipped to Lancashire and Cumberland ports, Glasgow, Ireland or North Wales. Boats also load for Gainsborough and Hull: for Sheffield, Lincolnshire, the East and West Ridings of Yorkshire, Newcastle and Edinburgh.

Source E

Forth and Clyde Canal

Canals
Navigable rivers

0 — 50 miles
0 — 80 km

Leeds and Liverpool Canal

Leeds

Liverpool

Hull

Bridgewater Canal

Manchester

Coventry Canal

Grand Trunk or Trent and Mersey Canal

Staffs and Worcs Canal

Birmingham

Oxford Canal

Grand Union Canal

Monmouth Canal

Bristol

London

Kennet and Avon Canal

Things to do

1 Read **Turnpike Trusts** and Source C. Why would manufacturers be willing to pay turnpike tolls?

2 Look at Source A. It is late; the weather is bad and the stagecoach is in a hurry. The toll-keeper wants money. Write a conversation between the toll-keeper, the coachman and the passengers. Don't forget to set the conversation in the early nineteenth century.

3 Why were canals built when the roads had been improved so much?

4 Read Source D. Use Source E to work out the routes Thomas Coleman's barges would have used to get people's goods to these destinations. Remember he was based in Birmingham.

Railways

The very first railways were on the coalfields, where horses pulled coal wagons along wooden rails. Coal mines had steam engines, too, but these were used to pump water out of the mine workings. Sometimes fixed engines were used to winch wagons along the rails.

The first steam train

It was Richard Trevithick, a Cornish mining engineer, who hit upon the idea of combining a fixed iron rail with a moving steam engine. In 1804 his steam engine pulled five wagons, a coach and seventy passengers from the Pen-y-Daren **ironworks** in South Wales to the Glamorganshire canal. However, Richard Trevithick did not have the money to develop his steam engine, nor could he find wealthy people to back him. He died, a poor man, in 1833. Others, however, realised the importance of what he had done. They took his brilliant idea and carried it further than even he could have dreamed.

A railway network

In 1825 a steam engine called *Locomotion* pulled a train from Stockton to Darlington. Five years later the Prime Minister, the Duke of Wellington, opened a railway between Liverpool and Manchester. He travelled in the train, pulled by an engine called *The Rocket*. It was a great success, even though, at the opening, William Huskisson, MP for Liverpool, was knocked down by a passing train and later died.

People rushed to put money into railways and many new lines were built. During this 'railway mania' some people lost thousands of pounds putting money into crazy schemes. However, by 1855 more than 8000 miles of track linked all the major cities in Britain and the railways were carrying more goods than the canals.

Arguments against the railway at the time.

- Canal transport would end.

- There would be soot everywhere.

- Turnpike trusts would go bust.

- Fox hunting would be ruined.

- Milking would be affected.

- Women would miscarry.

- Sparks would cause fires.

- There would be railway tracks everywhere.

- Fast travel would send people mad.

The Railway Station painted in 1862 by William Powell Frith.

Aberdeen

Dundee

Glasgow

Edinburgh

Britain's railway network in 1852.

| ⌇ **Railway** |

| 0 | 50 miles |
| 0 | 80 km |

Newcastle
Sunderland

Leeds

Liverpool

Manchester

Hull

Crewe

Derby

Birmingham

Norwich

Cardiff

Bristol

London

Exeter

Southampton

Portsmouth

Brighton

Dover

Things to do

1 What did Richard Trevithick do to help bring about the railway network?

2 Look carefully at Source F. Can you find a criminal being arrested? A porter carrying bags? What else is happening on the station platform?

3 Some people think that the growth of the railways led to the following:

- industry grew and developed
- iron and coal production soared
- people bought a greater variety of foods
- firms specialised in what they produced
- new towns grew up
- national daily papers were produced
- time was standardised all over Britain
- people went on holidays and day trips.

How many of these can you explain?

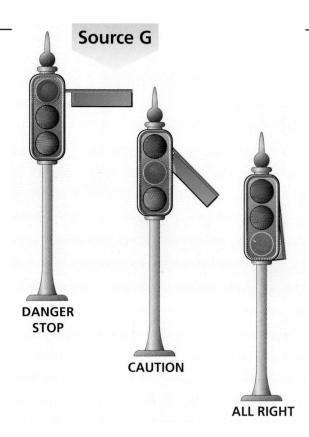

Source G

DANGER
STOP

CAUTION

ALL RIGHT

The standard signalling rules which Neele helped to develop.

George Neele, superintendent of the London and Northwestern Railway

George Neele worked in railways all his life. In 1846, aged 21, he was working for the Eastern Counties Railway at Ely as a clerk. Promotion came quickly. By 1862 he was superintendent of the London and Northwestern Railway, the largest of all the railway companies operating in Great Britain. He stayed there as superintendent until he retired in 1895. At his funeral in 1921, six London and Northwestern railway guards carried his coffin.

In 1904 George wrote a book called *Railway Reminiscences* in which he put down what he could remember of his working life. These extracts are taken from his book; some are in his own words (in *italics*) and some have been shortened.

Where's that train?

The sight of the steam by day and the headlight at night, or of the whistle of the approaching engine, formed the only means of information for the station master or porter who had to be on the look-out on the platform.

In the 1840s the telegraph was used on certain sections of some lines; the telephone was in fairly general use in the 1880s, but it was not until around 1910 that full traffic control systems were used on all main lines.

Signals

George Neele played an important part in developing a set of standard signals and signalling rules which were eventually accepted by all the British railway companies (see Source G).

Accident at Abergele, 1868!

George was on holiday at Lowestoft when the Irish mail train crashed outside Abergele in North Wales. He broke off his holiday to help with the investigation. An account of the accident was written in a letter to *The Times* newspaper by the Marquis of Hamilton, who was in one of the rear carriages with his wife and family. Here George writes about the letter:

He describes how immediately after the collision he got down from the train and saw the whole of the three front passenger carriages, the vans and the engines, enveloped in sheets of flame, and dense smoke rising 20ft high and spreading in every direction. The wreck was the work of an instant; not a movement of any sort, no struggle to escape, was apparent from the doomed carriages. Their contents of charred and mutilated remains were discovered an hour afterwards.

The Irish mail train had collided with four runaway wagons of petroleum.

A late nineteenth-century steam train.

Source H

Tourist train wrecked at Wigan, 1873!

For some reason the 16th carriage from the front broke away and, turning to the left, took with it the whole of the rest of the train. The first eight vehicles became a total wreck, with a terrible loss of life.

This accident was the first to be investigated by a public inquiry. The chief officials of the London and Northwestern Railway clearly thought the accident had been caused by speed. They believed they had to maintain high speeds because of competition from other lines.

Queen Victoria's train journeys

George Neele travelled with the Queen's train on her journeys to and from Scotland. Altogether he made 112 of these journeys.

1865
At Forfar, just as the Queen's train approached, one of the yardmen of the Scottish Northeastern took across the two main lines a goods wagon hauled by a horse, and had barely cleared the track when the train came up. Mr Esplin, the manager of the line, was in the Royal train, but the narrow escape did not appear to disturb him. All we could gather from him was that the yardman stated he did not know of the Royal train's coming: he had not noticed and went on with his work as usual.

1872
Passing along the platform in the dead of night at Wigan I was surprised to find John Brown (the Queen's servant) and on enquiring whether all was right, heard to my surprise, 'No! The Queen says the carriage is shaking like the devil.' But this certainly was only John Brown's way of putting it.

1884
On arrival at Oxford a note was received from the Queen complaining that gas had been introduced into the lights in her saloon instead of oil, and requesting an alteration. The substitution of oil then was impossible! The glare of the gas in the globes, which unfortunately were plain and not frosted, was the cause of annoyance, and I had the supply reduced as far as possible, to be of service.

Things to do

1 **a** What differences can you find between the London and Northwestern Railway and railways today?
  b Why do you think there are these differences?

2 The London and Northwestern Railway seems to have been quite dangerous!
  a What dangers can you spot in these extracts?
  b Would the signalling system that Neele helped to develop have made it less dangerous?

3 Queen Victoria seems to have found railway journeys somewhat troublesome. Why, then, did she travel by train?

We have seen how the Industrial Revolution affected people in Britain who worked in mines and factories and who had to live in industrial towns. But these were not the only people to be affected. There were changes, too, in the lives of the wealthy and their servants.

LADY CHARLOTTE GUEST

Lady Charlotte Guest was married to John Guest, who ran the Dowlais ironworks near Merthyr Tydfil, Wales. They married in 1833, when she was 21 and he was 48. Between 1833 and 1852 (the year John died) they had ten children. Lady Charlotte took an interest in the Dowlais works. The works made iron that was bought by railway companies and other industries. So Lady Charlotte was more involved in the Industrial Revolution than the wife of a country landowner would have been. But her diary, from which the following extracts come, are as full of parties and politics as they are of industry. Like many well-off women at the time, Lady Charlotte busied herself with working for the poor. She set up schools at Dowlais, both for the children of the workers and for the men.

Source A

Cynfarthfa Ironworks, painted in about 1870. Cynfarthfa was also in Merthyr Tydfil, and was owned by the Crawshay family.

Railways

Lady Charlotte and her husband travelled often. They usually went by coach, but they started to use railways more and more:
Then we caught the railway. We had two seats in the Mail part of the train. Our carriage was lashed onto a machine behind. We sent the servants to ride in that. The 36 miles took an hour and a half. By coach it would have taken us over four hours. It is much smoother and easier than a carriage and the speed is not alarming, because it is so steady.

Lady Charlotte laid the foundation stone for the Taff Vale Railway, on 16 August 1837:
I laid the mortar with a pretty little trowel. When the stone was lowered, the Engineer brought me an equally small hammer to strike it into place. I insisted on using a big wooden mallet, much to the amusement of the workmen.
Rail travel was not always as pleasant as Lady Charlotte's first experience. In July 1838:
I travelled part of the way home on the Great Western Railway. It is new, but rocked the whole way, like a steamship. There are many men already mending the line.

Factories

Interested people would visit factories regularly:

4 November 1833: We were up early this morning to see Mr Houldsworth's cotton factory, which he kindly showed us over.

I have never seen anything of the kind before, and was much pleased with the machinery. The process of passing the threads through a gas light, to take off the imperfections, is the prettiest part of the process. We then saw velvet embroidered by machine. We went, after, to Sharpe and Roberts's where there is all sorts of machinery. They were making a steam coach. A movable platform took people from the top storey to the bottom, instead of stairs. This is also a useful machine for loading wagons.

Cholera

Even outlying places, like Dowlais, were not free from the threat of cholera, which struck in 1849:

31 May: The cholera has broken out with great violence in Cardiff. John has been to a meeting about cleaning the town. Dowlais is to be whitewashed and cleaned as much as possible. The doctor has set up a system of house-to-house visits to check if anyone has the early symptoms.

9 June: The cholera is still raging, and has crept gradually to Gellivaelog, just across the river from Dowlais.

11 June: A letter from Dr White reports the first case of cholera at Dowlais. His visitors now have much to do on the house-to-house searches. People are so alarmed and frightened that many imagine symptoms that are not there. The doctors will be worn out before the cholera sets in.

22 June: The cholera is worse at Dowlais. Thirteen deaths a day. I have sent asking for more medical help.

31 July: The children and I are now in the country. The cholera at Dowlais is so bad. Twenty or more dying a day. Eight men constantly employed in coffin-making.

Lady Charlotte giving prizes at Dowlais school in about 1855.

Source B

Things to do

1 a How was Lady Charlotte's life affected by the Industrial Revolution?

   b Why might she have been more affected than some other wealthy women?

2 a What precautions did the Guests take against cholera in Dowlais?

   b Why do you think Lady Charlotte left it so long before moving away from Dowlais once cholera broke out?

Domestic service

The numbers of people working in factories rose rapidly during the Industrial Revolution. Even so, most women worked in **domestic service**. Most men worked in farming, but the second biggest employer of men was domestic service. Unlike factories and mines, no **commissions** were set up to investigate the working conditions of servants. No laws were passed about the age at which a child could go into service, or their hours, or wages. Servants were a fact of life. They had always been there, absolutely necessary to those who used them, but invisible. Did the Industrial Revolution affect them? It depended on their job and their employer.

HARRIET BROWN

In 1870 Harriet Brown, new in service, wrote to her mother:
I am up at half past five or six each morning and do not go to bed till midnight. I do the fires and just keep on, all day. I feel so tired sometimes I have a good cry. Mrs Graves the cook is very kind. She helped me with my work this morning, or I would never have got through it. I would like to ask you to visit next week, but we have two dinner parties and shall be ever so busy. I can give you plenty of mending, when there is time, but I do not know when that will be.

Twenty years later Harriet was a married woman sending her daughter Ellen into service. Ellen worked the same hours and cried herself to sleep, too. Those starting at the bottom of the servant ladder always had the hardest time of it.

Who were servants?

Domestic servants worked in other people's homes, doing the work that kept the house and garden running.

Rich people with huge houses and grounds could have over a hundred servants. Servants lived in their own part of the house or grounds and all had a particular job to do. There were men to open the front door, do the gardening and look after the horses. There were housemaids who dusted, cooks, and scullery maids who washed up. Important servants, like the butler and the lady's maid, had nothing to do with the boy who cleaned the boots and shoes or the girl who did the washing up!

At the other end of the scale, in poorer households, was the young girl who came in each day from her own home to help. She did everything, from cleaning to looking after the children.

Source C

The men who worked at Petworth House in the 1870s. They are (from left to right along each row, top to bottom) the assistant under butler, a footman, the under butler, another footman, the house steward, the lodge keeper, the chef, another lodge keeper, a footman, the steward's room man, the second chef and the final footman.

A servant's life was not always dull. Here a servant who left to marry has come back for a visit. Everyone has stopped for a cup of tea and a chat. It is unlikely that the cook, returning from her afternoon out, will approve!

Changes?

In the 1890s more people began to have labour-saving devices in their home, to reduce the work for servants. They also began to give servants more time off. They could have an afternoon at the cinema, or an evening at the **music hall**. Some servants even got a whole day off, so they could use **excursion trains** to have a day at the seaside or in London. More and more servants benefited from the changes brought by the Industrial Revolution. Why? Because by this time there was a shortage of servants. People who had once gone into service, especially women, found there were other jobs they could do which gave them more freedom and better wages; new jobs, created by new inventions. They could work at a **telephone exchange** or as a secretary, although they needed some education for these jobs.

WILLIAM LANCERLY

I began in service as a boot boy, aged sixteen. I had to clean boots and shoes, sharpen knives, fetch and carry, trim the lamp wicks (the house had no gas or electric), lay up and wash up for the servants' meals, clean the windows, mirrors and the silver and help to carry and wait when there were people to dinner. After two years I was made footman. After four years I was given a holiday, because the family would be away from home. I had three whole days. In this time I visited London, and decided to get a job with a family with a Town House there. So I did. My duties there were light, I was even given an evening off from time to time to go to the theatre. But there was no chance of promotion, so I moved on. When I eventually had to appoint servants myself, I found that farmers' children or servants' children were best because they were used to early rising and hard work.

Things to do

1 Use all the information on pages 70 and 71 to write a description of what it was like to be either:
  • a servant in a large house
  • a servant in a house with only a few servants.

2 a Make a list of the ways in which the Industrial Revolution might have affected the lives of servants.
  b Why did it affect some servants more than others?

3 We know that Lady Charlotte Guest had servants. List the ways in which they might have been affected by the Industrial Revolution.

In 1775, Britain's American colonies decided they had had enough of British rule. They drove out the British, wrote a *Declaration of Independence*, and set about working out how thirteen states with different laws and attitudes, not least of all to slavery, could work together as a 'nation'. Newspapers and speeches were full of ideas about '**liberty**' and 'the rights of man'. These ideas spread across the sea to Europe, which spent the rest of the century trying to cope with them.

Liberty and equality?

In many countries the gulf between rich and poor, between those with power and those without, seemed vast, with one law for the rich and another for the poor. When, in 1789, Paris exploded into a **revolution** that swept across France, some people saw it as a good thing. Conditions for many people in France had been appalling. The new government's *Declaration of the Rights of Man* (Source A) sounded perfectly reasonable. However, when the King and nobles who had 'oppressed the poor' were executed by the newly-invented **guillotine**, people abroad began to get nervous. A Revolutionary Government was set up to make sure reforms – including fixing the price of bread, and free education – were carried out all over France. But it soon became more concerned with keeping hold of power. It became more and more extreme, and sent people to the guillotine at an ever-increasing rate. What next? Would this unrest spread?

Source A

The main points of the *Declaration of the Rights of Man*, 26 August 1789:

- **Men are born free, with equal rights.**
- **No one should rule without the support of the people.**
- **All people can have a say in government, themselves or by a representative, who must explain his actions to them.**
- **One person's liberty must not hurt another's.**
- **People can only be arrested if they break the law.**
- **Everyone is innocent until proven guilty.**
- **People can have their own political and religious beliefs.**
- **Police will enforce the law, for the public good, not for their own gain.**
- **People will give money to run the country, according to what they can give. They must be told how it is spent.**

Monarchy (Louis XVI)	Revolutionary Government	Emperor Napoleon	Monarchy restored	Republic
1786	1794	1815	1830	1848 1849

The government of France 1786–1849.

A cartoon drawn in the 1790s showing possible effects of the French Revolution on the other countries of Europe.

Watching France

The rest of Europe watched France uneasily. It seemed that the events there were affecting the rest of Europe. The 1789 Revolution in France sparked off unrest in other countries. This was snuffed out, but left governments worried. When France was settled, Napoleon Bonaparte made himself emperor and began a series of wars trying to take over all of Europe. Later rebellions in France, in 1830 and 1848, often sparked risings in the rest of Europe. Most failed. Some, like Belgium's attempt to break away from Holland in 1830, succeeded.

What about Britain?

Britain avoided a revolution. The government made just enough reforms to keep people happy. Even so, when ordinary people held rallies and mass meetings about the right to vote, the government reacted sharply. If they left things too long, it could get out of hand – just look at France. When hungry agricultural workers marched, setting fire to hayricks, even farms, the government was even more worried. After all, rising bread prices had set the French Revolution going.

The government often reacted harshly. It sent a group of labourers from Tolpuddle to Australia for seven years' hard labour (see pages 24–5). Their 'crime' was not striking, or causing a riot, but joining a trade union. This was not actually illegal, so they were prosecuted for swearing an illegal oath instead. In 1819, magistrates sent armed soldiers to attack a crowd (which included women and children) at a meeting at St Peter's Field, Manchester about political reform. We know a revolution did not break out, but the government feared it was just around the corner.

Things to do

1 Draw a poster or cartoon to show the demands of the Declaration of the Rights of Man.

2 a What sorts of government did France try after the 1789 Revolution?
  b Why do you think they kept changing?
  c How did this unsettle the rest of Europe?

3 Why did Britain not have a revolution?

73

The thirteen British colonies in America were set up at various times, by different groups of people. They had their own local governments, laws, religions, even money. They squabbled with each other, especially over the boundaries between them. Yet by 1775 Britain had managed to make them so angry that they united to force Britain to give them **independence**. How did Britain so mismanage relations with the American colonies? Partly, it was reacting to a fear that it might lose the colonies to Britain's old enemy, France.

War with France

Britain and France both had colonies in America and in Canada. They both wanted to gain more land – from each other. In 1756 Britain and France went to war in America. The British colonies all sent soldiers to fight the French and when the British won, in 1763, the colonists went home expecting gratitude, even rewards. But Britain was determined to keep a tight grip on the colonies.

British interference

Instead of being grateful, the British passed laws that seemed mistrustful of the colonists. These laws stipulated with whom the colonies could, and could not, trade and doubled the taxes the colonists had to pay on goods from Europe. Britain told its colonies to set up armies or pay to keep a British defence force there. The colonies did neither. So, in 1765, Parliament set up a new tax, the Stamp Tax, to pay for a British defence force. Everything that was bought or sold had to have a stamp, which had to be paid for. The colonists refused to pay. They rioted. The British governors wrote frantic letters home and the Stamp Act was **repealed**.

Growing unity

Britain's laws applied to all the colonies. Each new law gave the colonies a greater sense of unity and shared injustice. As the British taxed more goods, the colonies organised and acted together. They refused to buy British goods. The British were forced to stop the new taxes, all except the one on tea. This started a riot in Boston. British soldiers, in a panic, fired on the crowd and five people were killed. The 'Boston Massacre' set off a stream of political pamphlets against the British.

The thirteen British colonies in 1775.

A painting of the Battle of Princetown, 3 January 1777. The man on the white horse leading the American soldiers on the left of the picture (the British are on the right, in red coats) is General George Washington.

The colonies set up a secret information network, ready to organise the war with the British which now seemed inevitable.

The war

British attempts to collect taxes led to protests. The British closed the port of Boston after the colonists dumped a shipload of British tea in the harbour (an event known as the 'Boston Tea Party'). Other places did the same. The colonists were becoming more openly defiant. The British closed the Virginian governing body to strike against colonial local government, so the Virginians set up their own government and a Congress of the States. The secret network was out in the open. The British army met at Lexington in 1775, to march on Concord, where there was a rebel arms store. The rebels in Lexington sent a message to the people in Concord to be ready. The war began. The rebels published a formal Declaration of Independence from Britain in July 1775. At first everyone thought the rebels would be beaten easily. But the war dragged on for six long years, until September 1781 when the British surrendered at Yorktown. In 1783 the official peace treaty was signed. The rebels had won. They could begin to become Americans.

Becoming American

The colonies had been united in their need to get rid of the British. But once rid of a common enemy, the states began to remember all the things that made them different. The governing body, Congress, could not pull them all into line. One man, Ethan Allen, made it clear that he and his men had fought for independence for Vermont, and that if they did not get it he would *retire to the mountains to wage war on all humanity.* He didn't. Instead he plotted with the British to make Vermont a British colony again, although this failed through lack of support. When Congress eventually drew up a plan for governing the states, it had to have two levels. Some decisions were made for all the states by Congress. But local matters were to be decided by state governments.

Things to do

An English visitor to America in 1759 said:
The colonies are jealous of each other. People have different manners, religions and interests.

a What pulled them together?
b Draw a cartoon to show the steps to unity against the British.

Paul Revere – hero of the American Revolution

Listen my children and you shall hear
Of the midnight ride of Paul Revere,

began a poem by the poet Henry Longfellow. The poem goes on to tell in great (sometimes inaccurate) detail how Paul Revere, hero of the American Revolution, took the news of the advance of the British army from Boston to Lexington, then Concord.

Who was Paul Revere?

Paul Revere was one of the early organisers of the 'Sons of Liberty' who spoke out against British taxes. He was a silversmith and engraver who also published anti-tax pamphlets. He was one of the riders who took news and messages from colony to colony as they organised themselves. He is said to have taken part in the 'Boston Tea Party' (where some of the Sons of Liberty, disguised as Indians, threw British tea into the harbour). He then took the news to other states. He set up a system of lantern signals to send a warning of the British army's advance.

What happened?

Almost everyone in Boston knew the British army intended to march. On 18 April 1775, they set off. Revere was rowed across the Charles River from Boston to Charlestown. He rode towards Concord. All along the way he woke people and warned them to be ready. A man called William Dawes was sent to do the same job by a different route. By midnight Revere was in Lexington where he met up with Dawes. They set off for Concord, joined by Dr Samuel Prescott, who lived in Concord but had been visiting his girlfriend in Lexington. Prescott is not known to have taken an active part in activities against the British before.

They met a British army patrol. Dawes escaped to Lexington. Revere was captured. His horse was taken from him and he was forced to walk back to Lexington. The final, vital, leg of the ride was made by Prescott, who jumped his horse over a fence and made it to Concord.

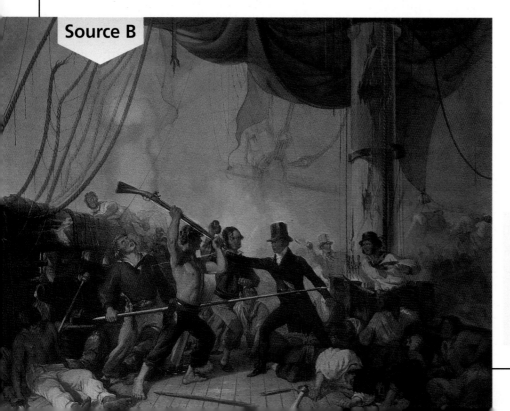

Source B

Even after the American Revolution, fighting, mainly at sea, continued between the British and the Americas. This picture, painted in 1815, shows one such clash.

Part of *Paul Revere's Ride*, by Henry Wadsworth Longfellow:

*Listen my children and you shall hear
Of the midnight ride of Paul Revere,
On the eighteenth of April in Seventy-five;
Hardly a man is now alive
Who remembers that famous day and year.*

*It was twelve by the village clock,
When he crossed the bridge into Medford
    town.
He heard the crowing of the cock,
And the barking of the farmer's dog,
And felt the damp of the river fog,
That rises after the sun goes down.*

*It was one by the village clock
When he galloped into Lexington.
He saw the gilded weathercock
Swim in the moonlight as he passed.
And the meetinghouse windows, blank and
    bare,
Gaze at him with a spectral glare
As if they already stood aghast
At the bloody work they would look upon.*

*It was two by the village clock
When he came to the bridge in Concord
    town.
He heard the bleating of the flock,
And the twitter of birds among the trees
And felt the breath of the morning breeze
Blowing over the meadows brown.
And one was safe and asleep in his bed,
Who at the bridge would be first to fall,
Who that day would be lying dead
Pierced by a British musket ball.*

*So through the night rode Paul Revere;
And so through the night went his cry of
    alarm
To every Middlesex village and farm,
A cry of defiance and not of fear,
A voice in the darkness, a knock at the
    door,
And a word that shall echo for evermore!*

Source C

Paul Revere's ride was still being sung about in 1900.

Things to do

1 a What did Paul Revere do to help the American Revolution?

  b What did Samuel Prescott do to help the American Revolution?

2 'Samuel Prescott was the hero, not Paul Revere. History should tell the truth.'

'Paul Revere did most of the ride. Prescott's involvement was accidental. It is fair for Revere to get the credit.'

Which of these statements do you think is more accurate? Explain your answer.

3.3 THE GIFT OF LIBERTY

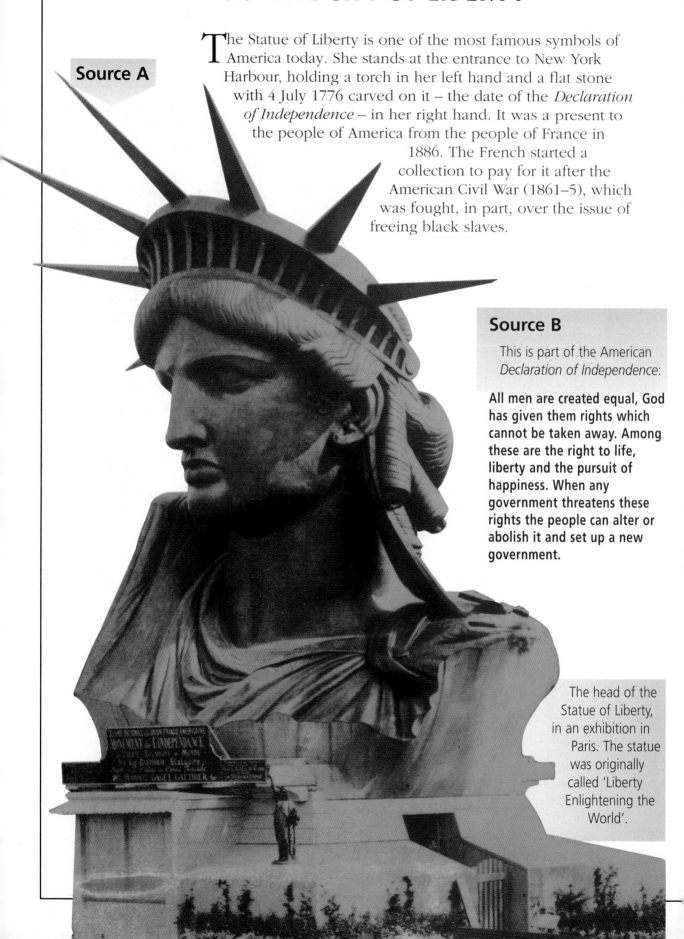

The Statue of Liberty is one of the most famous symbols of America today. She stands at the entrance to New York Harbour, holding a torch in her left hand and a flat stone with 4 July 1776 carved on it – the date of the *Declaration of Independence* – in her right hand. It was a present to the people of America from the people of France in 1886. The French started a collection to pay for it after the American Civil War (1861–5), which was fought, in part, over the issue of freeing black slaves.

Source A

Source B

This is part of the American *Declaration of Independence*:

All men are created equal, God has given them rights which cannot be taken away. Among these are the right to life, liberty and the pursuit of happiness. When any government threatens these rights the people can alter or abolish it and set up a new government.

The head of the Statue of Liberty, in an exhibition in Paris. The statue was originally called 'Liberty Enlightening the World'.

Why did they do it?

The statue was said to be a celebration of liberty. It was a reminder that the French had fought for liberty, inspired by the stand the Americans had made in 1776. It was also a congratulation to the winners of the Civil War, whom the French saw as fighting for liberty – the liberty of black slaves in the South. It was also a piece of advertising for France. It said, in 46 metres of beaten copper, 'we believe in Liberty'. The world may well have needed the reminder. Only a few years earlier, in 1871, the French government had put a stop to a revolution in Paris with great brutality.

Ideas and reality

The words at the foot of the Statue of Liberty say:
Give me your tired, your poor
Your huddled masses, yearning to breathe free,
The wretched refuse of your teeming shore.
Send these, the homeless, tempest-tossed to me.
I lift my lamp beside the golden door.

The words summed up America to many Europeans. It was a land of opportunity, a place where the poor, homeless and hopeless of an over-crowded Europe could make a fresh start, and prosper.

But by the end of the nineteenth century America was feeling overwhelmed by immigrants, especially the poor and homeless. By 1892 the steady stream was a flood. A new site was needed to 'process' immigrants. From this point on it got harder to enter the USA, although no official limits were placed on the number of people who could enter the country until the 1920s. They were inspected on the ship. Any with serious infectious diseases could not leave. The rest were shipped to Ellis Island, soon called 'the isle of tears' in several languages. At Ellis Island people were examined and inspected. Doctors chalked letters on their clothes to show if they had heart disease or rickets, or were feeble-minded. People with chalked letters on their clothes were taken back to the boats. The rest carried on being processed by officials, who were rushed off their feet. Those who finally got landing cards often entered America with a different name – the closest the official could get to their real one.

Source C

In 1852, a free black man, Frederick Douglass, was asked to give the 4th of July speech in Independence Day celebrations. The people who asked him were startled by his reply, which pointed out that many states still actively supported slavery.

Pardon me, and allow me to ask, but why am I called here today? This Fourth of July is yours, not mine. To drag a man in chains to the temple of liberty and call on him to rejoice with you – are you mocking me? Over your joy I hear the mournful wail of millions, whose chains, heavy yesterday, are made more unbearable by celebrations all around the nation today.

Things to do

1 a Why did the French give the Americans the Statue of Liberty?

b Why do you think the date on it is 1776, not the date of the end of the Civil War?

2 Read Source B. Frederick Douglass was a free black man, so why does he talk about being brought in chains to speak?

3 'People at this time talked a lot about liberty, but they didn't really believe in it. Look at the Americans. You get the *Declaration of Independence* and yet they've got slavery and they turn lots of immigrants away.'

Do you agree with the speaker?

Why did the French Revolution break out in 1789?

All kinds of causes

There was not one cause for the French Revolution. There were many. Some causes had been brewing for some time. Other causes were more recent. These long and short term causes all added together to make a revolution more and more likely, until it got to a point where anything could have set it off.

Rich and poor

The gap between rich and poor had been growing wider for years. It was most obvious in the cities, especially Paris, where the rich and poor lived side by side. Things were worse in years when the harvests were bad. Then there was not enough corn, so the price of bread went up sharply. The 1780s had several bad harvests in a row. The harvest of 1788 was the worst yet, and the price of bread had doubled.

Running the country

France was divided into three groups – the First Estate (churchmen), the Second Estate (rich and important people) and the Third Estate (everyone else, from rich shopkeepers to homeless beggars). While the Third Estate did the most work, they did not have a say in how France was run. But they were expected to pay taxes – more than the other two Estates.

ROBESPIERRE

Robespierre was part of the Revolution from its early days. At first, he seemed to support moderate reforms, as many people did at the time. It was not until late 1793 that he made it clear that he saw ruling by terror as a necessary way to govern. In the months that followed he became more and more suspicious of everyone, even his close advisers. It was the changes he made to the law, allowing people to be arrested if simply 'suspected' of a crime, that led his enemies to arrest and execute him in 1794.

The storming of the Bastille prison, 14 July 1789.

Source A

In 1789 the French king had to call the Estates General (a meeting of representatives of the three estates) because the government was in debt and he needed more taxes. Kings only did this when desperate for money – the last Estates General had been in 1614! When it met, the Third Estate demanded a say in how the country was run. The King refused. The cartoon shows what happened next.

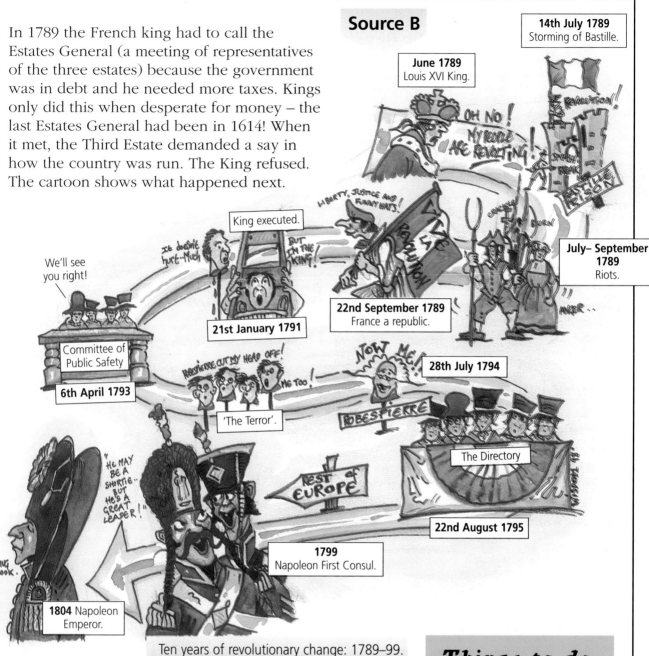

Source B

Ten years of revolutionary change: 1789–99.

What then?

After the fall of Robespierre, a more moderate government took control. In 1795 they set up the Directory, a five-man council that ran things with the help of Parliament. They undid most of the work of the Revolutionary Government, good and bad. They stopped any resistance by using the army. One army leader quickly became powerful. As the Directory relied on the army more and more, so his power grew. By 1799 he was powerful enough to throw out the Directory and take over France. His name was Napoleon Bonaparte. You can read about him on pages 84–7.

Things to do

1 Draw a spider diagram to show the causes of the French Revolution. Have a box in the middle, labelled 'The French Revolution, 1789'. Put boxes all around, with a cause in each box.

2 Shade long-term causes one colour. Shade short-term causes another colour.

What happened after the Revolution?

What was Paris like immediately after the Revolution?
An Englishwoman called Helen Williams lived there and
wrote a book about it. Here are some extracts.

Growing suspicion

From the moment the Revolutionary Government
came to power the atmosphere in Paris thickened
with growing suspicion. Every day fresh plots were
discovered. They were laid at the door of nobles,
priests, bankers and foreigners. Now that the
phrase 'suspected' came into use – you could be
arrested on suspicion of being involved in a plot,
with no proof against you at all. The members of
the Revolutionary Tribunal protested at the broad
sweep of this. They were accused of 'moderation'
and replaced with men who were willing to do as
they were told. The Revolutionary Government
also decided that revolutionary committees should
be set up all over the country to make sure their
decrees were carried out. There were fears that
the revolutionary committees in the countryside
might not be active enough, so a revolutionary
army was set up to go around the country,
checking up on the committees.

Imprisonment

Rumours abounded. We were told English
residents would not be harmed. Then we were
told we would be arrested and have our property
taken. The days passed. More and more of our
friends were arrested. Yet the local revolutionary
committee did not arrest us. We began to think
that, as a family of women, we would be spared.
But this was a time when neither age nor sex
won you compassion. We were woken in the
middle of the night by a loud knocking on the
door. Two soldiers and two representatives of the
revolutionary committee had come to arrest us.

Helen Williams should not have been surprised
that the Revolutionary Government acted
against the English, who had been against the
Revolution, even in its early days. This cartoon
was printed in England in 1792.

Source C

Un petit Souper, a la Parisienne: — or — A Family of Sans Culotts refreshing, after the fatigues of the day.

WHO WAS HELEN WILLIAMS?

Helen Williams was an Englishwoman who went to live in Paris in 1788, when she was 26 years old. She was in favour of ideas of liberty and equality that she found flourishing there, and wrote letters home saying so. She was friendly with many people who had wanted to reform France. She had approved of the Revolution. She was horrified when events got out of control. Many of her friends were executed. She wrote letters to the English newspapers about what was happening. This made her fear that she, too, would go to the guillotine as an 'enemy of the people'. She eventually escaped to Switzerland, returning when the Terror was over.

While Helen Williams told the truth about Paris after the Revolution as she saw it, she did gloss over the reforms made by the Revolutionary Government, like providing free education and fixing the prices of basic foods. This is hardly surprising because she was strongly against the Revolutionary Government.

A kind of freedom

My sister's French fiancé got us released. But we were watched. We went out little. We were terrified we would break some new law and get arrested. There were spies everywhere. We jumped at each knock at the door, fearing arrest. Prisons grew daily more crowded. More and more people went to the scaffold as the Terror tightened its grip. One person was arrested because he 'looked noble', another because a total stranger said he supported the monarchy. Some were arrested for being too clever, others for being too rich. Others were given no reason at all.

The guillotine

As the numbers of executions rose, the horrors increased. Stories of courage and cowardice passed from home to home. You heard of one person taking another's place on the scaffold to save them. Others were less courageous. Madame du Barry, once the mistress of the King, had to be dragged every inch of the way to the scaffold. The screaming seemed to go on forever. Paris was a slaughterhouse. The guillotine claimed innocent and guilty alike, at such a rate that the gutters seemed to stream with blood.

Rising terror

Robespierre seemed mad with power. No one, not even his closest friends, felt safe. We were told to leave Paris in ten days, or go to trial. This meant the scaffold. So we left. We managed to get special passes to return to Paris. This saved our lives for, soon after we returned, a decree was passed ordering all nobles and foreigners outside Paris to be executed. Paris itself was far from safe. You could be arrested 'on suspicion of being suspected' now. Most people watched the processions of death with stupefied horror. What could they do? They could not stop the executions. Even to show horror or sympathy would put their foot on the steps to the scaffold, their neck beneath the blade of the guillotine. Life was so difficult and dangerous that many killed themselves.

Things to do

1 **a** The time that Helen Williams is describing is often referred to as 'the Terror'. Why?

   b If it was so awful, why didn't people try to stop it?

2 How might the following people have justified their behaviour during the Terror:
   - a soldier
   - Robespierre?

3 The Revolutionary Government put Helen Williams in prison and executed some of her friends. Why should we believe anything she says?

3.5 NAPOLEON – EMPEROR OF FRANCE

Who was Napoleon?

Napoleon Bonaparte is perhaps France's most famous historical figure, but he was very nearly Italian and not French! The island of his birth, Corsica, was an Italian possession until 1768 when it was taken over by the French. One year later Napoleon was born, the second son of a local lawyer. He was raised speaking Italian, but was sent to be educated in France. He won a scholarship to the élite military school in Paris and took just one year to pass the two-year course.

When the Revolution broke out in 1789 Napoleon was in Paris. Four years later, he commanded the gunners defending the southern city of Toulon against an English attack. The Revolutionary Government was so impressed that he received several promotions (of course, some army officers had fled during the Revolution, so there were vacancies!). In 1795 he defeated a pro-Royalist revolt in Paris and was rewarded by being promoted to Major General. He soon won a series of battles against the Austrians and in 1798 defeated the Egyptians at the Battle of the Pyramids. Back in Paris people heard stories of the brave deeds of their great general and Napoleon became a household name.

Napoleon takes control

Whilst in Egypt, Napoleon heard that the government in France was having difficulties. He returned to Paris and soon decided that France needed stronger government. He convinced the Directory that he was loyal to it and was made commander of the troops in Paris. But really he was plotting against it, and two days later, on 11 November 1799 he used the army to seize power. The Directory was overthrown and replaced by a government headed by three **consuls**. Napoleon was to be First Consul, which really meant that he ran the country. This was shown five years later when he had himself crowned Emperor in the cathedral of Notre Dame in Paris.

Source A

Comments made by Napoleon during the preparation of the *Code Napoléon*.

The husband must possess the absolute power and right to say to his wife 'Madam you shall not go to the theatre, you shall not entertain such and such a person.' Women should stick to knitting.

Napoleon might have been Emperor of France, but that did not mean that he was exempt from everyday illness. Here is a list of his medical problems.

- Constipation and piles
- Pain when urinating
- Scars and pain from old battle wounds
- A disease which caused shrinking of the penis
- Stomach cancer (which eventually killed him)

A painting of Napoleon crowning himself Emperor in 1804. Napoleon has taken the crown and is placing it on his own head. The artist, David, was Napoleon's Chief Painter.

Napoleon in power

In 1789 Napoleon had claimed to support the Revolution, but though he is famous for his reforms there were many ways in which his rule was not in keeping with the ideas of 'liberty and equality'.

- Napoleon had himself crowned as Emperor. During the Revolution, the King had been beheaded.
- Napoleon also gave noble titles to his family and in 1808 created an Imperial nobility of senior French aristocrats. The Revolution had abolished the nobility.
- During the Revolution many churches were closed down and France 'de-Christianised'. Napoleon agreed to allow Catholics to worship openly once more, but he insisted that he, not the Pope, should appoint bishops.
- Although Napoleon allowed all men to vote, once he became Emperor there were no more elections.
- Napoleon did not allow freedom of speech. He censored newspapers and set up a secret police force to control his opponents. The Revolution had banned censorship, though it was used during the Terror (1793–5).

Things to do

1 Which do you think is more important in explaining Napoleon's rise to power: luck or his own ability?

2 Do you think it is true that Napoleon betrayed the Revolution?

3 What impression of Napoleon do you get from Source B?

4 If you were a historian writing about Napoleon as a ruler of France, would you say he was a great man?
(Concentrate on his laws. Don't include his skills as a warrior. That comes next!)

But Napoleon is known in France as a great reformer and some of his reforms were in keeping with the spirit of the Revolution.

- In 1804 he introduced the *Code Napoléon*. This was a clear statement of the laws of France. It said that all people were equal before the law and there were no special privileges for rich people. But it also said wives had to be obedient to husbands.
- Napoleon reformed the education system, placing more emphasis on science and mathematics and introducing a new type of school, the *lycée*, run on military lines.
- Napoleon wanted Paris to be a fitting capital for an emperor and spent money on new buildings in the city.

Napoleon the warrior

Napoleon is best remembered as a great military general who conquered almost all of Europe and made France the most powerful country in the world. When Napoleon came to power, France was at war with Austria, Britain and Russia. Napoleon defeated the Austrians at the Battle of Marengo in 1800 and forced them to sign a peace treaty agreeing that the French should control Holland, Switzerland and parts of Italy. Austria's allies, Britain and Russia, also made peace.

But by 1803 France was at war with Britain again. The British feared that Napoleon was becoming too powerful and that he intended to threaten the British Empire. Napoleon decided to invade Britain and put an end to its opposition to him. In 1804 an army was stationed along the French coast ready to invade. Napoleon had to be sure that his navy was strong enough to control the Channel and protect his soldiers as they crossed. But in October 1805 Admiral Nelson led the British navy to victory over a combined Spanish and French fleet at the Battle of Trafalgar. Napoleon decided to call off his invasion plans.

Source C

The rule of the Bonapartes in Europe.

France	– ruled by Napoleon
Spain	– ruled by Joseph (Napoleon's brother)
Holland	– ruled by Louis (Napoleon's brother)
Italy	– ruled by Eugene (Napoleon's stepson)
Westphalia	– ruled by Jerome (Napoleon's brother)
Gustalla	– ruled by Pauline (Napoleon's sister)
Lucca	– ruled by Elisa (Napoleon's sister)
Naples	– ruled by Joachim (Napoleon's brother-in-law)

Source D

The flight of Napoleon at Waterloo. His élite force of Old Guard are clearing the way for him.

Source E

A Russian general describing the condition of the French army during its retreat from Moscow.

I saw a dead man, his teeth deep in the back leg of a horse, which was still quivering. I saw a dead man inside a horse which he had disembowelled and emptied so that he could crawl inside it and get warm. I did not see the wretched French eating each other, but I did see dead bodies from whose thighs strips of flesh had been cut away for eating.

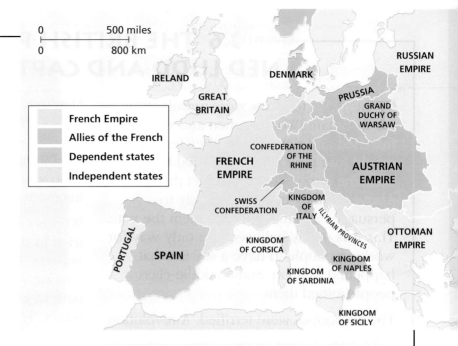

Europe in 1810.

Legend:
- French Empire
- Allies of the French
- Dependent states
- Independent states

Problems

In 1805 Russia, Prussia and Austria joined Britain against France, but they were soon defeated. By 1810 Napoleon controlled almost all of Europe. He set up the Continental System, forbidding countries under French control to trade with Britain. He wanted to force the British to make peace. But soon things started to go wrong.

In 1808 the King of Spain died. Napoleon decided to make his brother king instead of the rightful heir, Ferdinand. Soon France was at war with Spain and its neighbour, Portugal. Napoleon had expected this and thought that 12,000 men would be enough to win this Peninsular War. In the end he had an army of 300,000 soldiers and still lost. The British sent troops led by the Duke of Wellington to help the Spanish and by 1813 Napoleon's troops had been driven back into France.

More defeats

Napoleon invaded Russia in the summer of 1812, and reached Moscow in September. But as the Russians retreated, they burned everything of value – especially food. Soon Napoleon realised that he would have to pull out of Russia. As his men began their long retreat, winter fell and thousands died from the cold.

Napoleon had taken an army of over 600,000 men into Russia. Only 50,000 made it back to France.

Final defeat

By 1814 Napoleon's position was so weak that he was forced to surrender to his enemies. He was deposed and the old king's son was reinstated as Louis XVIII. Napoleon was sent to live in exile on the island of Elba off the coast of Italy. But he escaped in 1815 and returned to Paris. He was welcomed by huge crowds who wanted to see a return to the glorious days when France controlled Europe. But it was not to be. Napoleon was defeated by the combined forces of Austria, Russia, Prussia and Britain at Waterloo on 18 June 1815. He surrendered again and was sent into exile on St Helena, an island 8000 km from France. He died there in 1821.

Things to do

It is 1821. Napoleon has asked you to write his *curriculum vitae*. Write a list of headings (e.g. Place of birth, Education, Early work experience, etc.) and then complete his c.v.

In the years after 1832, leaflets demanding the six points of the People's Charter (Source A) appeared on the streets of Birmingham, Glasgow, Leeds, Liverpool and London. Why was this?

Many working people had hoped that the Reform Act of 1832 would give them the vote. The vote, they believed, was the only way to get a fairer deal for themselves. That way they could elect working people as MPs and their voice would be heard properly in Parliament. But they were badly disappointed. Parliament was still dominated by the wealthy. Many working people wanted change, and they wanted it quickly. So they gave their support to the People's Charter and became Chartists.

Who joined the Chartists?

People who became Chartists were craftsmen like printers and cabinet makers, factory workers like cotton spinners and home-workers like woolcombers, handloom weavers and framework knitters. Some who joined turned to Chartism only when times were bad. Others remained Chartists all their lives.

Source A

The People's Charter:

1 A vote for every man over 21 years of age

2 A secret ballot

3 No property qualification for MPs

4 Payment for MPs

5 Equal-sized constituencies

6 Annually elected parliaments.

The Chartists sent three huge petitions to Parliament which asked for the Charter to be granted. They said that the first petition (in 1839) contained one million signatures, the second (in 1842) contained three million signatures and the third (in 1848) contained six million signatures. Parliamentary officers looked carefully at the signatures on the last petition. They found signatures like 'Queen Victoria', 'Pug-face' and 'Flat-nose'. In this picture, the procession is taking the 1842 petition to Parliament.

Source B

Physical force Chartists

Holding rallies and collecting signatures on petitions are reasonably peaceful ways of making a point to those in authority. Not all Chartists thought this was the answer.

In 1839, after the first petition had been rejected by Parliament, Chartists in Halifax and Wakefield, Bradford and Leeds armed themselves with sticks, **cudgels** and sometimes guns and began practising drill in secret on the moors. Frightened of an armed rebellion, the government put General Napier in charge of 500 soldiers and gave him responsibility for keeping law and order in the north. In the same year John Frost led an armed gang of miners and iron-workers to release a fellow Chartist from gaol in Newport. Twenty-four people were killed in the battle which followed.

Source C

The Chartists had several leaders at different times and in different places. However, the two most important national leaders were William Lovett and Feargus O'Connor.

We have resolved to obtain our rights, peacefully if we may, forcibly if we must.
(Feargus O'Connor)

**Muskets are not what is wanted, but education and schooling of the working people.
Before an educated people a government must bow.**
(William Lovett)

Source D

This rather fuzzy photograph is the world's earliest known news photograph. It shows the Chartist rally on Kennington Common, London, in 1848. Chartists used rallies to help gain public support and to keep people aware of what they wanted.

Things to do

1 Read the six points of the People's Charter. Explain why the Chartists thought each point was necessary.

2 Look at Source B. How many reasons can you think of for Parliament turning down all three Chartist petitions?

3 a What different methods did the Chartists use to try to persuade people to support them?

   b Read Source C. How does this help to explain why the Chartists used so many different methods?

4 Design a Chartist poster to persuade people to support the movement.

5 Did Ned Ludd, Captain Swing, Rebecca or the Chartists pose the greatest threat to the authorities?

The period covered by this book was a time of great change. One woman who saw great change in her life during this period was Martha Carpenter.

The baby of the family

Martha was born on 7 August 1849 and was baptised Martha Handley Carpenter at the parish church in Datchworth, Hertfordshire when she was one month old. She was the baby of the family. In 1849 her brother George was eleven years old and her sister Emma was five. Two brothers had died: Thomas in 1841 when he was five months old and James in 1846 when he was just one month old. There were to be no more children after Martha.

Working parents

Martha's father, Edmund, was 32 and her mother, Eliza, was 38 years old when Martha was born. Edmund worked as a farm labourer but sometimes he said he was a dealer. In 1851 the whole family lived at Burnham Green. Later they lived at Bramfield (where Edmund was born) and at Woolmer Green. All these villages were 3–4 miles from Datchworth. Edmund and Eliza worked for local farmers and moved to wherever there was work. Maybe they went to annual hiring fairs in Hertford, the nearest town. There tenant farmers would inspect the labourers who were offering to work and choose the ones they wanted. Edmund would have dug ditches and mended fences, mucked out yards, ploughed fields, sowed seed and harvested corn. Eliza could have worked in the fields, too. Or she may have worked indoors, making cheeses and butter, smoking bacon and hams, baking bread and brewing ale.

Source A

Datchworth parish church, where the Carpenter family were baptised as babies and where most of the family were married and buried. Martha's brothers Thomas and James, who died before Martha was born, were buried here. So was her brother George, who died aged 49, and her sister Emma, who died aged 50. Martha's father was buried here in 1880 and her mother in 1888.

Source B

From the *Daily News*, 1891:

You cannot go far along country roads just now without meeting wagons piled up with the goods and chattels of farm-hands moving home. They have been to some hiring fair and have got fresh places and here they are jogging about the country with their tables and chairs and beds and boxes and wives and children heaped up on the new master's wagon.

Things to do

1 Use the information on this page to draw up Martha's family tree.

2 Read these two descriptions of Martha's life as a girl.
'Martha lived a healthy life in the open air, working in the fields, and when she was old enough, she got a job where she was able to better herself.'
'Martha had a dreadful life working in the fields and then was sent away from home to work for other people's children.'

Use the information in this unit to explain with which description you agree.

Source C

At harvest time, before machinery, the whole village turned out to help, as you can see in this photograph.

Source D

Memoirs of life as a farm-hand, by Tom Mullins. Tom was a farm-worker born in about 1863.

A man could cut half an acre of corn a day and bind it into sheaves, but usually the farmers banded themselves together and worked in groups of from twelve to twenty.

How country folk laughed when the first machines appeared. Some mowing machines were used as reapers, with a dozen men following behind, binding the cut corn. Men were paid sixpence for a bundle of 24 sheaves. We tried ploughing using a long wire and two stationary steam engines; it made a rough job but was quicker.

When I was seventeen I earned £16 a year and my keep. Bread was three pence a quartern loaf, milk three pence a quart, tobacco three pence an ounce, while beer was two pence a pint, the best was three pence.

School or work?

Martha did not go to school and neither did Emma or George. Even if Edmund and Eliza had wanted to send their children to school, they could not have afforded to. In 1880 an Act of Parliament made it compulsory for all children up to the age of ten to attend school, and eleven years later this elementary education was made free. But this was far too late for the Carpenter children. Martha remembers working in the fields when she was three or four, scaring the birds away; then, when she was older, having to weed between rows and rows of vegetables for hours. One day she was so hungry that she pulled a turnip from the ground and ate it raw.

Going up in the world?

When Martha was about twelve years old, she went to work in the 'big house' which was in a nearby town. She joined a team of servants as a nursery maid, and her job was to help the nanny and the nurse look after the children. A governess had been hired to teach the children and Martha was determined to learn to read and write, too. Using the children's books when they were asleep, she slowly and steadily taught herself.

When Mr and Mrs Steels from London came as visitors to the house, they were impressed by this little nursery maid who seemed anxious to better herself and get on in life. Mrs Steels needed a lady's maid and offered Martha the job. So, in 1867, Martha, with her belongings in a tin box, set off for London and a new life.

Martha the lady's maid

Source A

Martha went into service with the Steels family. As Mrs Steels' lady's maid, she lived in the Steels' house, in Hammersmith, London. Mr Steels was a strict Anglican and insisted that all his employees were **confirmed** as members of the Church of England. And so when Martha was 20 years old, she was confirmed at St Peter's Church, Hammersmith.

In the 1860s and 1870s London was an exciting, bustling place. Horse-drawn cabs, butchers' carts and delivery wagons thronged the cobbled streets. The pavements were crowded with rich and poor: bankers and businessmen, flower-sellers and crossing-sweepers, ladies with their maids and children with their nannies, beggars and prostitutes. It was a very different place from the muddy lanes of Datchworth.

We don't know how long Martha stayed with the Steels. We do know that she went out with a young man called George Henry Crane, who was 'in service' as she was. George was a Londoner, but he had a country background. His parents, Henry and Ann, were born and spent their childhood in Norfolk, and he had uncles, aunts and cousins living there when he met Martha. On Christmas Day 1876, Martha and George were married at the Holy Trinity Church, Islington. Martha was 27 years old and George was 24.

This photograph of Martha was taken when she was Mrs Steels' lady's maid. The clothes she is wearing are far too posh for a maid! When her mistress was out one afternoon, Martha simply borrowed one of her dresses, put it on and went and had her photograph taken.

Married life

Shortly after George and Martha married they went to live in Islington with George's parents, Henry and Ann, and George's unmarried sister, Eliza, who worked in a local factory making fancy goods. Few houses allowed women to continue as servants when they married and Martha had to stop being a lady's maid, although she probably took on temporary work.

Things to do

1 Look back at the family tree you drew. Use the information on these two pages to complete it.

2 Look carefully at Source B. The photograph is not dated. How would you set about working out when it was taken?

3 When a person dies, they might have an obituary written by a friend or a colleague. This would give an account of the person's life and also give some idea of what the person writing the obituary thought about the dead person. Write an obituary for Martha.

Martha with two of her daughters, Alice and Agnes.

George started to work with his father as a brewer's **drayman**. George and Martha had four children: Alice Elisabeth in April 1878; Henry James in October 1880; Agnes Harriet in June 1883 and Rose Martha in February 1889. Henry James was to die of TB in 1900, but the three girls lived long lives and were all over eighty years old when they died. Agnes was to marry Albert James Woolfe, the grandson of George and Maria Woolf. You read on pages 46 and 47 about Maria's dreadful death from cholera.

At some point Martha and George moved to a larger house in Islington. They took in lodgers – and together ran the pub at the end of the road. All four of their children went to elementary school, where they learned to read, write and do basic arithmetic. When they left, the girls trained as seamstresses and were all given treadle sewing machines as 21st birthday presents. Henry (whom the girls nicknamed 'Boy') was too ill to work.

Martha and George stayed in Islington until George died in 1928. Martha was to live for another 29 years and saw her great-granddaughters ride bikes, watch TV and join the Brownies – all unheard of when Martha was a girl.

Source C

Martha aged 96 years old. This photograph was taken in September 1945 just after the ending of the Second World War. Martha was living in Northampton with her daughter Alice, who was widowed in 1940, and her daughter Rose, who never married. Martha died in 1947 when she was 98 years old.

The changing world

The twentieth century has been a time of upheaval and very rapid change. As the maps on these two pages show, the world in the 1990s is very different to the world as it was at the beginning of the century. The major powers no longer own huge empires in Africa and Asia and almost all of the old colonies have gained independence.

World powers in 1900

In 1900 the richest and most important powers were Great Britain, Russia, France, the USA, Germany, Austria Hungary, Italy and Japan.

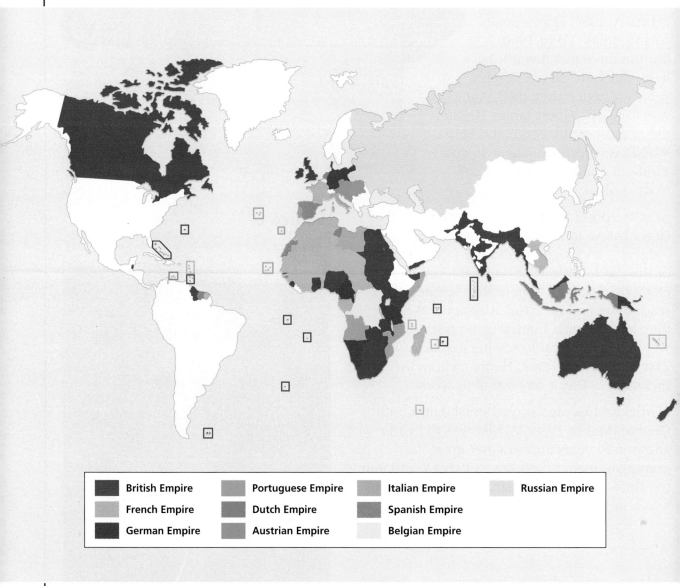

British Empire	Portuguese Empire	Italian Empire	Russian Empire
French Empire	Dutch Empire	Spanish Empire	
German Empire	Austrian Empire	Belgian Empire	

The world in 1900.

From colonies to trade

At the end of the twentieth century, the power of a nation is measured not by how many colonies it has, but by how much influence it has on world affairs. This influence comes mainly as a result of a country's wealth. The United States, for example, is the most influential country in the world, and is also the wealthiest.

World powers in the 1990s

In the 1990s the countries with the largest share of world trade were the USA, Germany, Japan, France, Italy and the UK. The richest countries were Switzerland, Japan, Finland, Luxembourg, the USA and the United Arab Emirates.

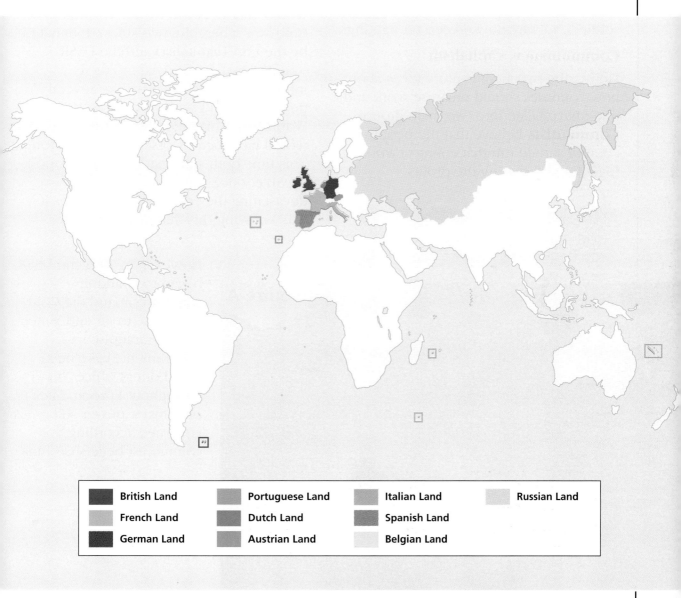

■ British Land	■ Portuguese Land	■ Italian Land	■ Russian Land
■ French Land	■ Dutch Land	■ Spanish Land	
■ German Land	■ Austrian Land	■ Belgian Land	

The world in 1997.

Always at war?

The twentieth century has seen two major world wars (1914–18 and 1939–45). It is also true that in almost every year of the century there has been war in some part of the world. Even as you read this there are many places in the world where fighting is taking place. One question you need to consider as you read this book is why are there so many wars? We know that warfare today kills innocent civilians as well as soldiers, so why do we keep on fighting?

Communism v. capitalism

During the twentieth century ideas about how countries should organise work and trade have fallen into two main groups:

Communists believe that the people in a country should run that country, working together and sharing the profits.

Capitalists believe that there should be workers and bosses. The bosses provided the capital (money to set up factories and workshops) and so get all the profits.

This argument spilled over into how countries should be ruled, too. After the Second World War ended, in 1945, the governments of countries took one side or the other. They did not trust each other. They felt that, sooner or later, one belief would take over the world. This led to a Cold War where the two sides, dominated by the USA (capitalist) and the USSR (communist), tried to extend their influence as much as possible. Several times the world seemed close to a Third World War. This time, the destruction would have been worse than ever before. This time both sides had nuclear weapons capable, once war broke out, of devastating the entire planet. Perhaps it was knowing this that held both sides back.

However, in 1991 the USSR began to abandon communism and the Cold War came to an end. Since then communist governments have been voted out of office throughout Europe. The only major power still governed according to communist beliefs is China.

Many modern wars are civil wars, fought with conventional weapons. Here soldiers of the Angolan government question a possible rebel.

Source A

A shrinking world

Conflict and mistrust have been big issues in the twentieth century. But there have been more positive issues too. Medical discoveries meant that diseases that were killers in 1900 are now easily treated. People have also worked together in technological research. In the 1900s there were still areas of the world unexplored. Now people can survey the whole world from satellites in space, and are exploring space itself. They can communicate with places on the other side of the world, almost instantly, using satellites.

The developing world

Many of the poorest countries in the world are countries that broke away from European empires, and could not develop their economies quickly enough to support themselves. The contrast between their poverty and the wealth of 'developed' countries has led to them being called 'the Third World', because life there is so different. Many people in these developing countries hover on the edge of starvation much of the time. They have much shorter life expectancies and little to cushion them if they are hit by natural disasters, like floods or droughts. Despite help from some developed countries many people in developing countries do not have clean drinking water, access to medical care, or anything like enough to eat.

1900–1998

World population

1900	1998
160,000,000	5,925,770,871

Average life expectancy

1900		1998	
Men	45	Men	73
Women	48	Women	79

Life expectancy, 1998

Republic of San Marino (highest)
(developed country)   85
Rwanda (lowest)
(in Third World)   36

Source B

Things to think about

Think about the things we use in everyday life that were not widely used in 1900. For example, how would your life be affected without:

electric light and power, central heating, computers, TVs, videos, music centres, batteries, planes, cars, motorways, cinemas, fast food, washing machines, dishwashers, microwaves.

In the 1990s it is easier than ever to talk to people and collect information from all over the world, especially using computer technology.

Why was there a war in 1914?

The war that broke out in 1914 had been brewing for a long time. The most powerful countries in Europe were rivals for power. Who had the biggest empire? Who was selling the most iron? Who was building the most ships? Could they stay in front? Would they have to fight to stop someone else taking part of their empire? As soon as one country started to build up its army and navy, the others felt they had to do the same. They formed alliances with each other, promising to help each other if war broke out. They made plans about what to do if they were invaded. In 1914 there were two sides:

The Triple Alliance: Austria-Hungary, Germany and Italy.

The Triple Entente: Britain, France and Russia.

Source A

The spark for war?

Europe was tense, ready for war. Once war broke out, the alliances would make sure that all the major powers became involved. On 28 June 1914 Franz Ferdinand, son of the Austrian emperor, was shot in Sarajevo, Serbia. Serbia was in the Balkans, a part of Europe that Russia and Austria-Hungary had struggled over for years. Serbia was friendly with Russia, not Austria-Hungary. A Serb shot Franz Ferdinand. So Austria-Hungary invaded Serbia. Russia was ready to help Serbia. Germany was ready to help Austria-Hungary. France had agreed to help Russia. Britain held back, hoping not to get involved. Italy too was uncertain what to do. Finally, in 1916, it joined the war against Germany and Austria-Hungary (it hoped to gain land from Austria-Hungary at the end of the war).

The first move

Kaiser Wilhelm II, the German ruler, felt his army and navy were better prepared than those of his enemies. He declared war on Russia on 1 August and on France two days later. He had to defeat France quickly before Russian troops were ready to attack his eastern border. So he decided to invade France. To do this he had to cross Belgium. In 1839 Germany and the other major powers had signed a treaty promising not to invade Belgium. The Kaiser asked the Belgians to let his army march through to attack France. Belgium refused. The Kaiser felt that he had no choice. He invaded Belgium on 3 August 1914. Britain declared war on Germany the next day, saying that Belgium needed protecting. Really the British were fighting to stop Germany becoming too powerful. Countries in the Empire such as Canada and New Zealand also joined the war on Britain's side.

A pre-war Italian cartoon, showing the Kaiser as greedy for an empire.

Where did they fight?

The Western Front

Germany's war to the west. Here Germany fought Britain, France, their colonies and (after 1917) the USA.

The trenches were on the Western Front.

Battle of Jutland

The only big battle at sea. Neither side a clear winner.

The Eastern Front

Germany's war to the East. Here Germany fought the Russians. There was no fixed line of battle here, the front line shifted back and forth over many miles. The Russians fought while they were also having a revolution which replaced their king with a communist government.

Submarines

The Germans used submarines to sink ships bringing supplies to Britain and her allies. When they sunk the *Lusitania*, a US passenger ship that was also carrying war supplies, the USA decided to join the war against Germany.

The Middle East

The war in the Middle East revolved around which side controlled the Suez Canal, which joined the Mediterranean to the Red Sea.

Italy

In 1914 Italy had been on Germany's side. In 1915 the Italians changed sides. So Germany had to fight Italy, too.

The Colonies

There was also fighting in the German colonies in Africa. The 3 colonies marked here were captured by the allies.

Who had what in 1914

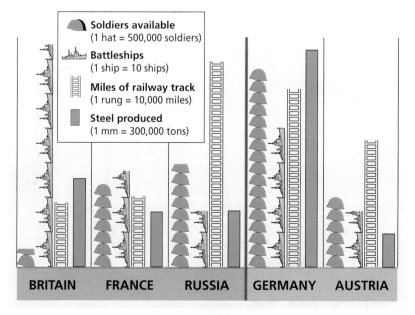

Soldiers available
(1 hat = 500,000 soldiers)

Battleships
(1 ship = 10 ships)

Miles of railway track
(1 rung = 10,000 miles)

Steel produced
(1 mm = 300,000 tons)

BRITAIN   FRANCE   RUSSIA   GERMANY   AUSTRIA

Things to do

1 a Who sided with whom in the first World War?

   b Can you explain why these countries sided as they did?

2 Look at **Who had what in 1914**. Which country was the most powerful?

3 Draw a diagram or cartoon to show how and when countries joined in the war. Begin with 1 August 1914.

The Liverpool Scottish in the trenches

The Liverpool Scottish Battalion were a territorial battalion – they were formed to protect Britain from invasion, not fight abroad. But they were soon swept up into the fighting on the Western Front. Robert Scott Macfie's letters home (in *italics*) let us follow the battalion through training, the first days in the trenches and the battles of Hooge and the Somme.

Numbers of soldiers killed, wounded or missing in three major offensives		
Verdun (1916)	French:	550,000
	German:	434,000
Somme (1916)	French:	200,000
	German:	500,000
	British:	420,000
Third Battle of Ypres (1917)	British Empire	310,000
	German:	300,000

Source E

Robert Scott Macfie.

The beginning

Today we have been told to be ready to go abroad on Friday 30 October. We are nowhere near ready: we have damaged rifles, many men are short of clothing and equipment. Headquarters is in confusion, lots of us are recruits and the rest are imperfectly trained. I never saw so incompetent a set of officers.

On 2 November they set off, jammed into a boat that, twelve hours after leaving England, was *going round in slow circles outside Le Havre.* They then had a long, slow, crowded journey to their training camp in France, but a long way from the front line.

Trenches

We have had our first practice digging trenches. They are not at all what I imagined and must be most uncomfortable in hot weather. I expect the scientific Germans will put in hot water radiators before the cold weather comes.

Moving up

We moved to a little village and joined the remains of several regiments which have been almost wiped out. The farm where we are staying is a sea of mud, ankle deep, and the roads are like rivers of yellow soup.

Christmas 1914

It is Christmas Eve and we are all very homesick. The men are in an empty barn, cold and draughty, and have hardly recovered from our spell in the trenches.

We have been able to dry our wet clothes, and even beat off some of the baked-on clay, but we are dispirited. We are waiting to march off to even less comfortable lodgings, 'dug-outs' – holes in the ground badly roofed and full of straw.

We went into the trenches cold and wet, for there was heavy rain and snow as we marched there from our muddy farm. When we came out we were colder, wetter and ever so much muddier. We must have looked like Siberian exiles, not soldiers. We wear whatever we can get, not smart uniforms, and have buckets and enamel cups and mugs tied to our belts with string. We do not march, we slouch along. We hang our heads and go along at irregular intervals in twos and threes. Many of the men fall behind, because they are lame.

The Liverpool Scottish, in action at Hooge.

Hooge (1915)

The attack at Hooge began on 16 June 1915. Macfie was in charge of the camp:

We got ready for the return of the troops. We set out letters, parcels, candles and food. We got tea and pea soup going on the cookers. 130 of my company had left: I was ready to feed them when they got back.

At last we heard the distant sound of pipes and after a while a handful of men came through the gate. Their uniforms were tattered, their faces blackened and unshaven, their clothes stained red with blood and yellow with the fumes of gas. I shouted for Y Company – only one man came forward. It was heartbreaking. Gradually others tottered in, some wounded, all in the last stages of exhaustion. By 5.30 a.m., six hours after they had all marched out, there were 25 of my men in camp. Since then I have found out that 11 were killed and 68 are in hospital. 25 are missing. I fear most are dead.

The Somme (1916)

A year later the Liverpool Scottish were involved in one of the most famous battles of the war – the Somme.

Our attack, in the early hours of 9 August, was directed against a village which has been attacked several times before, and several times since, always without success. Our performance was no exception: of my company 177 went up [joined the battle] – 20 were killed, 42 wounded; about 8 are missing, probably dead. The lack of preparation, the vague orders, the ignorance of what we were supposed to do, even of the geography of the place, the absurd haste, the horrid mistakes – it was all scandalous. After two years of war it seems that our higher commanders are still without common sense. In any well-run organisation one of the divisional commanders would have been shot for incompetence – here they just send another regiment to do the same job in the same muddling way. It is worse than Hooge, much worse – and it is still going on.

For King and country

When the war broke out, the British army had about 164,000 men. By 1916 there were over 2,000,000. Men went off to fight, for their king, for their country, and to defend 'gallant little Belgium'. Everybody wanted to be involved in this war against the bullying Germans. Or did they?

Against the war

Some people were against the war. Some of them didn't want to fight a war against Germany. Some were pacifists – they felt all war was wrong. They had a hard time of it. The government was trying to get all men to join up. Ordinary people would stop men who weren't in uniform as they walked down the street and ask why they were not in the services (army, navy and air force). Sometimes they even handed them white feathers, a sign of cowardice.

Source A

TO THE

YOUNG WOMEN OF LONDON

Is your "Best Boy" wearing Khaki? If not don't **YOU THINK** he should be?

If he does not think that you and your country are worth fighting for—do you think he is **WORTHY** of you?

Don't pity the girl who is alone—her young man is probably a soldier—fighting for her and her country—and for **YOU.**

If your young man neglects his duty to his King and Country, the time may come when he will **NEGLECT YOU.**

Think it over—then ask him to

JOIN THE ARMY TO-DAY

Conscription

Casualties were high in the war. Despite the huge intake of volunteers, more men were needed to fight. So the government brought in conscription in 1916. They passed a law that all single men aged 18 to 41 had to join the services. Later they made married men join up, too. Men who were doing important war work in Britain did not have to join up. The government also said that men with a 'conscientious objection' to the war (beliefs that stopped them from joining up) did not have to go.

'Conchie' or coward?

Conscientious objectors had to go to a **tribunal**. This was supposed to listen to their arguments and decide if they were really 'conchies' or just 'cowards'. In many cases the tribunal was just a way of trying to bully people into joining up. There were about 16,000 conscientious objectors. Many refused to fight but went to war as ambulance drivers, hospital workers and stretcher carriers. About 1500 of them refused to have anything to do with the war at all. Some of these were sent to prison. Others were forced into uniform. If they still refused to fight, they were tried for treason. Some were sent to prison. Others were shot.

Pressure to join up

The government put constant pressure on men to join up. Government posters told men to protect their country and their families. They told women to make their men join up. They even suggested that those who did not join up were making the war last longer, because if they joined up, the war would end and the killing would stop.

A poster pressurising women to get their boyfriends to join up.

ONE 'CONCHIE'S' WAR

Howard Marten was living in London at the start of the war. He was a Quaker, and Quakers did not believe in fighting. He registered as a conscientious objector. He was forced to join the Non-Combatant Corps (who did not fight, but worked at jobs like driving ambulances, instead). He and a group of others were put in prison in Harwich for refusing to obey orders. They were then shipped out to France. This made their position very dangerous. Disobedience 'in the field' was punishable by death.

Marten and four others were court-martialled for disobedience. Marten was surprised at the sympathy of those running the trial. Perhaps they were too sympathetic – the verdict was never announced and there was a re-trial. They were led out to the parade ground to hear their fate:

There were lots of men lined up, mostly Non-Combatants and labour battalions. We were taken to one side of it, then led out, one by one, into the middle of the square. I was the first of them and until my verdict was read, no one knew what was going to happen. An officer in charge read out the various crimes: refusing to obey a lawful command, disobedience at Boulogne and so on, then: 'The sentence of the court is to suffer death by being shot.' There was a pause. I thought, 'Well, that's that.' Then he said 'Confirmed by the Commander-in-Chief'. 'That's double sealed it now,' I thought. Then, after a long pause: 'But commuted to penal servitude [prison] for ten years.' And that was that. What was good was that we were back in England and out of the hands of the army.

Marten was sent to prison, then he was released to do useful war work in a stone quarry at Dyce, near Aberdeen.

Howard Marten, photographed with his mother and Cornie Barret, one of the other 'conchies' sentenced to death with him.

Things to do

1 Write down these words and what they mean:
 • pacifist
 • conscription
 • conscientious objector.

2 Read about Howard Marten.
 a Why was he a conscientious objector?
 b Choose two of the following people and say what they might have felt about Marten's sentence and why:
 • his mother
 • the mother of a man of his age killed on the Western Front
 • a man of his age who had been conscripted and had gone to fight.

Deserters and mutineers

If there was one thing worse than a conchie, as far as the army was concerned, it was a deserter (a soldier who ran away) or a mutineer (a soldier who rebelled against his officers). Yet the realities of the war, the inept way it was conducted and the horrific loss of life meant that many people who began by supporting the war turned against it.

Covering up

The government was furious when people who had been in battle turned against the war. They didn't want people at home finding out how bad things were. Everyone had to pretend, put on a brave face. Soldiers who went home on leave often felt very isolated. They had seen the realities of war, but in Britain most people were still talking about a different war, one that ignored the harsh realities of bad commands, appalling conditions and senseless waste of life.

This painting, *The Harvest of Battle*, was painted by the war artist C. W. R. Nevison. He made sketches at the time, but the painting was not finished until 1921. He would probably not have been allowed to show it in war-time.

SIEGFRIED SASSOON

Siegfried Sassoon was the generals' worst nightmare. He joined up as soon as the war started. He became an officer and led his men bravely into battle. He was given the Military Cross medal.

But Sassoon was appalled at the way the generals threw away lives for what he thought was no good reason. He wrote poetry about the horrors of war. In 1917 he threw away his medal. He refused to fight any more. He wrote to *The Times* newspaper, saying:
I am making this statement as an act of defiance of military authority as I believe the war is being deliberately prolonged by those who have the power to end it.

The army didn't want to court-martial a soldier who had won a medal. They tried to get Sassoon to tone down his criticisms. They excused him by saying that he had shell-shock from battle. They put him in a military hospital in Scotland, until he 'recovered'. While the army hoped he would 'come to his senses', Sassoon tried to get support for his anti-war views. But he felt more and more guilty about being 'out of it' while men were fighting and dying, so he returned to the front and survived the war.

Source C

An Australian recruiting poster. Troops from all over the colonies fought in the war. Some of them, like the Canadians, accepted the British army could court-martial their men. Others, like the Australians, did not.

Who was shot?

Three hundred and forty-six men were shot for military offences between 1914 and 1916. Most of them were ordinary soldiers. Three were officers. Many of them had been at the front for many months, had fought and suffered in the trenches, and one day just snapped.

Why were they shot?

The army shot deserters and mutineers as a lesson to everyone else. They had to make it more dangerous to run away from battle, or refuse to go into battle, than it was to take part. The lists of those shot were read out to all soldiers 'on parade'.

Source E

Captain Slack was an officer in the East Yorkshire Regiment. He had to organise at least one firing squad.

There was one poor little man who came to me. He was posted to my Company, ran away, was caught and ran away again, deserted, and he was court-martialled to be shot. My Sergeant-Major and I had to pick ten men to shoot him, which we did, and one of my officers had to be in charge with a revolver.

The man was shot. I wrote to his mother 'killed in action'; I think that's what they were all told. I wasn't at the execution. I didn't want to be. It wasn't a nice job for the ten men, either. My Sergeant-Major organised it. I didn't go into the details, if he was put on a chair and blindfolded, or the mark over his heart, I didn't go into the details at all. It was a horrible thing to have to do, but it had to be done.

Things to do

1 Why did the British army shoot deserters and men who refused to obey orders?

2 Read Source E. Write a letter home from the Sergeant-Major describing what happened and how you feel about it. Include what Captain Slack did.

3 The war has ended. There is a newspaper debate as to whether it was right to court-martial and shoot men for military offences. Write a letter to *The Times* about this from either:
   • an ordinary soldier who had seen men shot
   • a general
   • Captain Slack
   • the wife of a man shot for desertion.

Who were the suffragettes?

Suffragettes was the name given to women who demanded the right vote in elections. (Suffrage means being allowed to vote.) There were many different groups, who did not always agree about the best way to get support. The National Union of Women's Suffrage Societies (NUWSS), set up in 1897, wrote letters to MPs and held dinners to try to get support. They believed in convincing people gradually. Individual politicians gave them some support, but Parliament was very divided on the issue of votes for women and no-one considered it very important. In 1903 the Pankhurst family set up the Women's Social and Political Union (WSPU). Their motto was 'Deeds Not Words'. They were nicknamed 'suffragettes', a name which soon applied to all women demanding the vote.

What did they do?

The WSPU wanted publicity. They had a uniform of purple, green and white. They went on marches, held public meetings, printed their own newspapers. They went to factories and mills to speak to ordinary women. They got noticed. More and more women joined; old and young, rich and poor. But Parliament did not give them the vote. So the suffragettes did things to get arrested. They felt, rightly, that people would be shocked at them being treated as criminals. They got more support, but not the vote. Some became more militant. They smashed shop windows, set fire to pillar boxes, even homes (as long as they were empty). This lost the movement a lot of support. Many of their members felt they had gone too far and resigned. By the time the First World War started, suffragettes had become very unpopular.

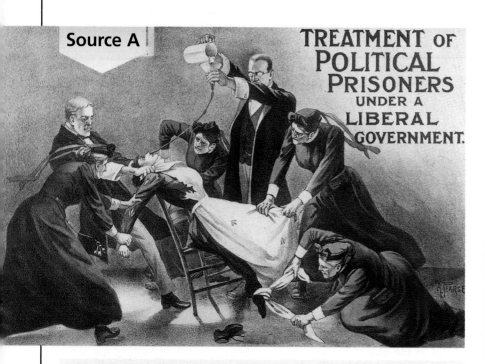

Source A

TREATMENT OF POLITICAL PRISONERS UNDER A LIBERAL GOVERNMENT.

Some of the suffragettes went on hunger strike in prison. The government said they should be forcibly fed, through a tube up the nose. This action horrified many people and gave suffragettes more support.

Things to do

1 What did suffragettes want?

2 a Who set up the WSPU?

 b How was it different from earlier movements?

 c Make a WSPU poster, using their colours, to tell people different ways they can support the movement.

3 An MP's home has been burned down by a suffragette. You are a suffragette asked to write a paragraph for the local paper about this. Are you a militant? Do you approve? Why?

Source B

The suffragette movement would not have succeeded without all the women who marched, sold papers and got arrested. These women are demonstrating outside Buckingham Palace on 21 May 1914.

THE PANKHURSTS

Emmeline Pankhurst and her daughters, Christabel, Sylvia and Adela, set up the WSPU. They took the lead in most of the activities of the movement, including being arrested. Christabel was one of the first to urge militant action.

The Pankhursts did not always agree over tactics. Sylvia and Adela wanted to push harder for working women to be given the vote. Emmeline and Christabel argued that it was more important to get the vote for some women first. This was best done, they argued, by getting the vote for the 'respectable' women who made up most of their membership. Working women who wanted the vote could not campaign in work hours. They also had the most pressure from their bosses and their families not to become suffragettes. This disagreement led to Sylvia being thrown out of the WSPU in 1914. Adela had already been talked into leaving when she became ill and kept losing her voice through all the public speaking.

FREDERICK PETHICK-LAWRENCE

Not all men were against women getting the vote. Frederick Pethick-Lawrence, a lawyer, advised the suffragettes on their legal rights, helped edit the newspaper *Votes for Women* and helped set up their printing business. He and his wife were arrested several times. He went on hunger strike and was force-fed.

EMILY DAVISON

Emily Davison is one of the most famous suffragettes. She gave up her teaching job to campaign full-time for votes for women. Emily was a militant. She smashed windows and set fire to pillar boxes. She was arrested several times, went on hunger strike and was force-fed. In 1913 she went to the Derby, a famous horse race held each year. She ran onto the racetrack to try to stop the king's horse, Anmer. She was trampled and died in hospital four days later. The suffragettes said she had died for the cause and gave her a huge funeral. Sylvia Pankhurst described her as *one of the most daring and reckless of the militants*.

113

What did people think of suffragettes?

Different people felt very differently about suffragettes. You cannot say 'men thought this' or 'women thought that'. People also changed their minds about suffragettes as suffragette tactics changed. Many people did not feel strongly either way.

Suffragettes and people who were against them fought hard to convince people to join their side of the argument. Militant people on each side could get very heated. Anti-suffragette posters suggested that suffragettes were frustrated women who could not get a husband, using the slogan *You don't need the vote, you need a bloke!* Militant suffragettes burned churches as well as houses. They also damaged famous paintings to make their point.

Source D

A SUFFRAGETTE'S HOME

VOTES FOR WOMEN

AFTER A HARD DAY'S WORK!
Published by the Campaign Committee, National League for Opposing Woman Suffrage, Caxton House, Westminster. JOIN!

Source C

An extract from *The Unexpurgated Case Against Woman Suffrage*, by Sir A. E. Wright, printed in 1913.

Failure to recognise that man is the master, and why, is at the root of the suffrage movement. Suffragettes ignore man's superior strength, so they ignore the fact that government runs on compulsion. They ignore man's superior mind, so come to think that they can think as well. They ignore man's superior money-earning capacity, so ignore the power of the purse.

Source E

From *The Times* newspaper, covering an election in 1909.

The suffragettes seem to have made a favourable impression on the voters here, especially the miners. Some miners would even vote for the candidate who was in favour of women's suffrage without thinking about his opinions on other subjects. This is the first election in which I have seen the voters really concerned about the right to vote – worried about the concerns of 20 or so women who are good speakers.

A poster from the time, made for the National League for Opposing Woman Suffrage (NLOWS). Women, as well as men, joined this league – just as men, as well as women, supported the suffrage movement.

Source F

Opinions on suffragettes in 1913.

Things to do

1 a In which three ways does the author of Source C say that men are superior to women?
  b How is Source D saying suffragettes are wrong?
  c Which source(s) would you use to show that not all men were against women?

2 Pick one of the people in Source F. Write down the argument you would use to make this person change his or her mind about suffragettes.

Needed at last!

When the First World War broke out, men joined the army in huge numbers. Women were needed to do the jobs these men had done. They were also needed to work in factories making guns, tanks, bombs and uniforms. And they were needed to nurse the wounded. Some women volunteered straight away. But more were needed. Suddenly the government needed the organisational skills of the suffragettes.

The Right to Serve

The government gave Mrs Pankhurst £3000 to organise women to do war-work, especially in the factories making bombs and bullets. The WSPU organised marches with new banners. 'The Right to Vote' became 'The Right to Serve'. Women took on the work that needed doing. All kinds of women worked, though poor women usually got the worst jobs. Women mined coal, made bombs, learned to be builders. They drove buses, cleaned windows and farmed the land. Hertha Ayrton invented a fan to clear gas from the trenches, so saving many lives. Women showed that, given the chance, they could do hard physical work, think as well as men and earn a wage, despite what critics said. Things would never be the same again.

Once more, the government was faced with campaigns for the right to vote. They gave in for many reasons. They wanted women to give men their old jobs back after the war, without a fuss. They had seen what women were capable of doing, so it was hard to argue that they were not capable of voting.

In 1918 all women over 30 were allowed to vote. This was extended in 1928 to women over 21, giving them the same voting rights as men.

A Right to Serve march, 17 July 1915.

Source G

TWO SUFFRAGETTES IN WAR

Source H

In August 1914, aged 18, Mairi Chisolm rode from Scotland to London, on her motorbike, to look for war-work. She got a job carrying messages for the Women's Emergency Corps (WEC), then went to Flanders as a nurse. The team of four doctors, four nurses, two ambulances and two drivers worked hard, but they were far from the front line. Wounded men died of shock on their way to be treated. So Elsie Knocker, a qualified nurse, and Mairi set up a first aid post just behind the front line in Belgium.

We were there for the Belgian casualties but we also had to try to rescue the pilots who were brought down in No Man's Land. That was what we got the Military Medal for, you see. We went on foot. There weren't always stretchers, we had to hope to get them out with their arms around our necks. I strained a valve in my heart lugging men around on my back. The Belgian army ambulances were three miles behind us. But we had an ambulance of our own and I'd drive them back up in that. It was like being a grouse being fired at, you had to do it in stops and spurts, being shot at. You had to get the timing right.

As well as dealing with the wounded, we got men in from the trenches with boils, sore feet, all sorts of things. We slept in our clothes, ready for when the wounded came in. We went into the trenches too – poked our noses in to see that everything was all right.

Mairi Chisolm and Elsie Knocker in Belgium.

CAROLINE RENNLES

Caroline Rennles worked in London, making bombs. The TNT in the bombs had a strange effect:

It turned the hair that stuck out from our caps ginger and our skin yellow. They used to call us 'canaries'. Some people were nice to us, but others used to treat us like scum. You couldn't wear anything nice to work, the powder got into it. It wore off, eventually. We didn't realise it was dangerous. Train conductors used to say 'You'll be dead in two years'. So we said 'We don't mind dying for our country'. We were so young and patriotic.

Things to do

1. **a** What sort of women did war-work?
   b What did they do?

2. **a** Why did some suffragettes help?
   b Why did some suffragettes not help?

2. Do you think women would have got the vote if they had not helped in the war? Explain your answer.

1.5 THE TREATY OF VERSAILLES

When a war finishes, countries have to meet to decide what is going to happen to the losers. Will they have to pay compensation to the winners? Will they have to give up land? Or could they even be taken over by the winning side? Of course, after all the killing and damage that has occurred in a war it is very difficult for decisions to be made calmly and in the best interests of everyone involved. The Treaty of Versailles which followed the First World War is a good example of this.

In January 1919 representatives from 32 countries travelled to France to decide what should be done about the defeated nations – Germany, Austria-Hungary, Turkey and Bulgaria. The representatives met in the Palace of Versailles in Paris and their discussions took six months. None of the defeated nations was allowed a say at the conference. They had to accept what was decided. Nor was Russia invited to send representatives. There had been a revolution in Russia in 1917 and the new leaders had made peace with Germany in return for giving the Germans huge areas of land. The Russians had dropped out of the war and had set up a communist government. The victorious Allies were angry about both of these things.

How were decisions made?

Although many countries were represented at the Versailles Conference, the decisions were really made by the three most powerful leaders. 'The Big Three' were Woodrow Wilson of the United States, Georges Clemenceau of France and David Lloyd George of Great Britain.

Wilson
Wanted a lasting peace and no more war.

Clemenceau
Wanted revenge on Germany.

Lloyd George
Wanted Germany punished but not too harshly.

Things to do

1 **a** Who were the 'Big Three'?
 b What different views did they have about what should happen at Versailles?

2 Look carefully at what was decided about Germany in the Treaty of Versailles.
 a Which leader do you think would be most happy with what was agreed?
 b Can you explain the reason behind each of the individual decisions made about Germany?

3 Why were some countries excluded from the talks at Versailles?

4 'The resignation of the German Chancellor didn't do much good, so his actions were pointless.'
 Explain whether you agree with this statement.

5 If you were the German Chancellor making a speech about what was wrong with the Treaty of Versailles, what would you say?

Source A

Harold Nicholson, who was one of the British representatives at the Conference of Versailles, made this comment after the treaty was signed:

The historian, with every justification, will come to the conclusion that we were very stupid men.

A major problem at Versailles was that the leaders had different ideas about what should happen. Wilson hoped that he could set up a fair peace and return to the United States with no risk of future war in Europe. Clemenceau, however, wanted revenge for the killing and damage that had happened in his country (where much of the war was fought). Lloyd George also wanted the Germans to be punished, but was worried that if the treaty was too harsh, the Germans would want revenge and another war would break out in the future.

▨ Territory lost by Germany to other countries	▨ Area formerly owned by Russia
▨ Territory lost by Germany to the League of Nations	▨ Demilitarized zone
▨ Area formerly Austria-Hungary	

Europe after the Treaty of Versailles.

What was decided?

The boxes below show the decisions the peacekeepers made. Neither the Germans nor any other defeated power had any say in what was decided. When the Germans saw the proposals, their Chancellor (leader) resigned in protest. But they were told that if they did not sign the treaty, the Allies would invade their country. On 28 June 1919 German representatives signed the Treaty of Versailles, but that was certainly not the end of the story!

The Treaty of Versailles

- Germany was to agree that the war was all its fault.

- Germany was to pay **reparations** for the damage caused (later fixed at £6600 million).

- Germany was to lose its colonies, and parts of the country were to be given to other European nations. (One effect of this was to split Germany in two.)

- The German army was to be reduced to 100,000 men (eleven million Germans fought in the war). It was to have no airforce, no tanks or submarines and only six battleships.

- Germany was not allowed to keep soldiers or build fortifications within 50 km of France.

- The lands Russia gave to Germany were taken away to form new countries.

Other decisions

- Austria-Hungary was divided into two countries.

- Yugoslavia and Czechoslovakia were set up (the peacekeepers wanted to let people of the same race govern themselves).

- Turkey lost almost all the land that it held in Europe.

The years following the First World War were dramatic to say the least. **Democratic** government came to an end in Germany; Mussolini established himself as **dictator** in Italy; and Russia saw the murder of its royal family and the setting up of a communist government.

The Romanovs

Until 1917 Russia was ruled by a royal family called the Romanovs. The head of that family was Tsar Nicholas II. He ruled Russia with the help of nobles appointed by him as advisers, but the 95% of Russians who were peasants or town workers had no say in how Russia was run.

The Tsar and his nobles lived a life of luxury. Everyone else did not. Much of Russia's farmland did not produce enough food and industrial workers in the towns worked very long hours for very poor pay. Despite this, many Russians loved their Tsar, whom they saw as chosen by God to rule. But in the latter half of the nineteenth century opposition to the Tsar began to grow in Russia and various revolutionary groups were formed. The Tsar responded by having his secret police keep a careful eye on opposition.

Revolution

In 1905 there was an attempted revolution against Nicholas. He was so concerned that he agreed to make changes. He even agreed to set up an elected parliament, called the Duma. But once Nicholas was confident that he was back in control, he took little notice of the Duma and carried out harsh measures against his opponents.

In 1914 Russia went to war against Germany. At first people welcomed the war, but as the army began to suffer defeats, discontent grew. The Tsar went to the front to lead the army. But this left his wife (a German) and her 'holy man' Rasputin to run the country. The Tsar became even more unpopular and a group of nobles murdered Rasputin.

A new government

By March 1917 there were riots in the streets and the Tsar was forced to **abdicate**. A new Provisional Government took over, but in October 1917 it was overthrown by members of the revolutionary party, the Bolsheviks.

RASPUTIN

Rasputin was a Russian peasant who saw himself as a 'holy man'. He had some interesting views, such as believing that people could only repent if they first sinned properly! Rasputin had tremendous influence over the Tsarina because he seemed to be able to help her son, Alexei, who suffered from a blood disease called haemophilia. But he was hated by the Russian nobles, who murdered him. First they poisoned him; then they put him in a sack and threw him in a river – just to make sure!

A poster issued by the Bolsheviks during the First World War. It shows the Tsar, the Church and the Russian nobility riding on the shoulders of ordinary Russians. All around are Russia's war-dead.

Source A

The Bolsheviks, led by Lenin, had great difficulty getting themselves established in power. To do so, they had to murder the Tsar and his family, and win a civil war against their opponents, who received support from most Western countries (who feared the Bolsheviks' political beliefs). Eventually Lenin changed the name of Russia to the Soviet Union and his party to the Communist Party.

After Lenin's death there was a power struggle between Stalin and Trotsky for control of the party. Stalin was eventually successful and Trotsky was exiled (and later murdered). Under Stalin, the Soviet Union was transformed into one of the world's two 'superpowers'. Yet there was a price to pay. Stalin hated any opposition. As many as 20 million people may have died for opposing his rule.

Events in Italy

Whilst a communist dictatorship was being set up in the Soviet Union, Mussolini was establishing himself as dictator in Rome. Unlike in the Soviet Union, where Lenin and Stalin said their eventual aim was to give the workers power, Italy's dictatorship was **fascist**. Mussolini did not believe the workers should have power. He said the people should make sacrifices for the good of the nation. Amongst those sacrifices were giving up the right to trade unions and free speech.

Italy after the First World War was a country of high unemployment, strikes and demonstrations. Many people feared there would be a communist revolution. Mussolini promised strong government and was anti-communist. His support grew. In 1922 thousands of his supporters marched on Rome and demanded that Mussolini be made Prime Minister. King Victor Emmanuel agreed and appointed Mussolini.

Gradually Mussolini took more and more power. Soon he ruled, not the King. He locked up opponents and banned other political parties. He did make some improvements in Italy's agriculture and industry, but is perhaps best remembered for his foreign policy. He was determined to create an Italian empire like that of the ancient Romans. He dragged Italy into the Second World War to support Hitler and was eventually humiliated by the Allied forces. In April 1945, Mussolini was murdered and he and his mistress were strung upside down from a lamp-post in Milan.

Benito Mussolini, Italy's 'New Roman Emperor'.

Things to do

1 Why do you think many people in Russia in the early twentieth century were unhappy?

2 If the Russian people were unhappy, why did so many of them still like the Tsar?

3 Make a list of the things that helped make the Tsar unpopular in the period 1905–17.

4 Why did Mussolini rise to power in Italy?

5 Why was entering the Second World War such a mistake for Mussolini?

Postwar Germany

After its defeat in the First World War, Germany faced many difficulties. The harsh terms of the Treaty of Versailles caused widespread resentment in the country and the cost of reparations added to the economic problems caused by the cost of fighting the war.

Shortly before the war ended, the German Emperor, Kaiser Wilhelm, had abdicated and left the country. Germany was to have a new constitution which said that it was now to be a **republic**. Since that constitution was drawn up in the town of Weimar, historians talk of the period in Germany after the war as one when Germany was governed by the Weimar Republic.

The Weimar Republic faced many difficulties in its attempts to bring about recovery after the war:

Source C

A poster issued by the Nazis showing Hitler as the saviour of Germany.

- It had signed the hated Treaty of Versailles. It had no choice, because the Allies had said they would invade if the Germans did not sign, but that did not stop the German people from blaming the government.

- There were several attempts to overthrow the government. In 1919 there was an uprising by a group of Communists called the Spartacists. It was put down only after fierce fighting. Then in 1920 Dr Wolfgang Kapp took control of Berlin and the government was forced to flee to Stuttgart. Control was only restored because trade unions in Berlin called a general strike and no one supported Kapp.

Finally, in 1923, a young German called Adolf Hitler, and his Nazi Party, tried to carry out a *putsch* (takeover) in Munich. It failed and Hitler was sentenced to five years' imprisonment.

- Perhaps the Republic's greatest problems were in finding the money to make **reparations** payments. In 1923, after failing to persuade the Allies to reduce the payments, the government decided to stop paying them. It was trying to convince the Allies that it could not afford the payment.

The French were so angry that they sent troops into Germany's main industrial area, the Ruhr, and took coal and other products to make up for the missing payments. Encouraged by their government, the German works went on strike. The German economy collapsed and a period of **hyper-inflation** broke out. Soon people's life savings were hardly enough to buy a week's groceries!

Fortunately for Germany, Gustav Stresemann became Chancellor in 1923. He introduced a new currency, the rentenmark, and ended inflation in Germany. He also restored relations with other countries. The French left the Ruhr and in 1926 Germany joined the League of Nations. The USA lent Germany money to build up its economy and by 1928 the problems of the postwar years seemed to be a thing of the past.

What the National Socialist (Nazi) Party believed

- The Treaty of Versailles should be torn up.
- Germany should have strong government.
- Germany should expand its territories into eastern Europe.
- The German race ('Aryans') are a master race.
- No Jews should be allowed to be Germans.

Crash

But in 1929 the American stock market collapsed and America went bust. It needed the Germans to repay the loans it had made. As a result many German businessmen went bankrupt. Similar problems occurred across the globe as the world tumbled into **recession**. Unemployment rose from below a million to over six million in Germany and the 'bad old days' of the early 1920s seemed to have returned.

Many Germans decided that the time had come for strong government. They turned to Hitler's Nazi Party. Here was a party which promised strong government. It said it would tear up the Treaty of Versailles, recover Germany's lost land and provide jobs. This was a popular message with the German people and when the Nazis won the most seats in the German Reichstag (Parliament) in 1932, Hitler was appointed Chancellor, taking office in January 1933.

Things to do

1 What reasons can you find on these two pages to explain why:
 a the Weimar Republic was unpopular
 b Adolf Hitler became Chancellor of Germany?

2 a What message do you think the Nazis were giving in Source C?
 b What things can you see in the poster which help get this message across?

3 It is January 1933. Adolf Hitler intends to tell the Reichstag why he will be a good leader. What do you think he will say?

Chancellor Hitler

The German people had voted for Hitler and his Nazi Party because they wanted strong government. They were not to be disappointed. Over the next two years Hitler established a **totalitarian** state in Germany. This means that the government had control of all aspects of people's lives.

The Enabling Act

Shortly after becoming Chancellor, Hitler persuaded the Reichstag (Parliament) to pass the Enabling Act, which gave Hitler the power to make laws and decide matters of war and peace for four years without consulting the Reichstag. In fact Hitler kept those powers permanently.

To make sure that he had full control in Germany, Hitler also banned all opposition parties and even had some of his own party murdered. The Nazis had their own private army, called the SA (Brownshirts). Hitler was concerned that the leader of the SA, Ernst Röhm, was becoming too powerful, so he had him and other leaders killed. Instead of the SA, Hitler used an élite group of the army, the SS, and the state police, the Gestapo, to root out and punish any opposition. During Hitler's time as Führer (leader), thousands of political opponents were sent to labour camps.

The harshest treatment was reserved for the Jews. Hitler used the Jews as **scapegoats**, blaming them for all of Germany's problems. He passed laws that took away their citizenship and forbade marriage (and even sexual intercourse) between Jews and Aryans (people with 'pure' German blood). Some Jews left Germany, but many did not get out in time and suffered the appalling fate of Hitler's Final Solution to the 'Jewish problem' (see pages 62–7).

'The young belong to me'

One of the ways that Hitler maintained his support was by using **propaganda**. The German people were subjected to a constant barrage of pro-Nazi propaganda on the radio, in the newspapers and in posters in the street. They even set up a special department led by Joseph Goebbels, called the Ministry of People's Enlightenment and Propaganda, to ensure that people 'got the message'.

But Hitler's main concern was the young of Germany. He knew that many German adults already had strong views on how Germany should be governed. The young, however, did not yet have such views, so they could be trained to think the way the Nazis wanted. This was what Hitler meant when he said that Germany's children belonged to him.

A timetable from a girls' school in Nazi Germany.

Source D

Periods	Monday	Tuesday	Wednesday	Thursday	Friday	Saturday
8:00 – 8:45	German	German	German	German	German	German
8:50 – 9:35	Geography	History	Singing	Geography	History	Singing
9:40 – 10:25	Race study	Race study	Race study	Ideology	Ideology	Ideology
10:25 – 11:00	Recess, with sports and special announcements					
11:00 – 12:05	Domestic science with maths	Domestic science with maths	Domestic science with maths	Domestic science with maths	Domestic science with maths	Domestic science with maths
12:10 – 12:55	Eugenics	Health Biology	Eugenics	Health Biology	Eugenics	Health Biology

allen Störenfrieden!

Einheit der Jugend in der
Hitlerjugend!

A fund raising poster for the Hitler Youth.

Source F

Part of a newspaper article written by David Lloyd George, who was British Prime Minister at the Conference of Versailles, after meeting Hitler in Germany in 1936:

I have just returned from Germany. I have now seen the famous German leader and also something of the great change he has made. Whatever one thinks of his methods – and they are certainly not those of a parliamentary country – there can be no doubt that he has achieved a marvellous transformation in the spirit of the people, in their attitude towards each other and in their economic outlook.

One man accomplished this miracle. He is a born leader of men. He is also securing them against the constant dread of starvation, which is one of the worst memories of war and the first few years of peace.

At school, children were taught that the Führer was a great leader who should be obeyed, that Aryans were a superior race and that the Jews were to blame for all Germany's problems. Even the history books were re-written to prove this. Of course, teachers had to belong to the Nazi Teachers' Association and were dismissed if they would not join.

Education was not only for the mind. There was plenty of physical education so that boys would grow into healthy men for the army, and girls would be fit for motherhood.

Outside school, youth organisations were set up to reinforce these views. At the age of six, boys joined the Little Fellows, at ten they went on to the German Young Folk and at fourteen they joined the Hitler Youth, where they were trained as soldiers.

Girls joined the Young Maidens at six and at fourteen the League of German Maidens. They were left in little doubt that their role in life was as wives and mothers. Hitler did not approve of women going out to work, or wearing make up. But if you had lots of babies, you were awarded a special medal, the Motherhood Cross.

Things to do

1 a What is a totalitarian state?
  b What evidence can you find on these pages to suggest that this was what Hitler set up in Germany?

2 Read Source F.
  a What does Lloyd George say were Hitler's achievements?
  b Do you think Hitler improved Germany or made it worse? Explain your answer.

This means war!

Hitler told the German people that he intended to tear up the Treaty of Versailles and regain the land that had been taken from Germany. He also said that he intended to win land from countries in eastern Europe (whose Slav population he considered inferior) and settle German people there. Such policies were bound to lead to war, but the other Western powers were reluctant to risk war by stopping Hitler's aggressive policies, so it was not until 1939 that war finally broke out.

Hitler's actions

In 1933 Hitler withdrew Germany from the League of Nations – a peace-keeping organisation set up after the First World War to try to prevent such a terrible war happening again. But to succeed, the League depended on its members being prepared to take action to stop a country that launched an attack on another country. In 1931 Japan had attacked China, but the League had been unable to stop Japan capturing the Chinese province of Manchuria. Two years later Mussolini attacked and captured the African state, Abyssinia. Again the League could not prevent the takeover. Hitler's withdrawal from the League showed that he did not have peaceful intentions, but the League could do nothing to stop his plans in the next few years.

Hitler soon began breaking the terms of the Treaty of Versailles. He reintroduced conscription and began building up the German airforce (the Luftwaffe).

Britain and France did little to stop him because they thought that Germany had been unfairly treated at Versailles and a strong Germany would be a good counter to the Soviet Union (Hitler hated communism).

In 1936 Hitler sent his troops into the Rhineland. This was part of Germany, but the Treaty of Versailles had said that Germany must not have troops in it. Hitler was very worried about the reaction of Britain and France and told his generals to withdraw if there was any opposition. But Britain and France did not want to risk war by opposing what Hitler had done. They protested, but took no action. This merely increased Hitler's confidence that he could do as he wanted without having to fear the consequences.

Germany's gains 1933–9.

Germany in 1933

Territory gained by September 1939

North Sea
Baltic Sea
EAST PRUSSIA
GERMANY
March 1936
Sept. 1939
Polish Corridor
March 1939
March 1935
POLAND
Rhineland
Sept. 1938
Sept. 1939
Saar
Sudetenland
FRANCE
CZECHOSLOVAKIA
March 1938
AUSTRIA
SWITZERLAND
HUNGARY
ITALY
N
S
0   200 Miles
0   300 km

Failure of appeasement

Resentment of Versailles Treaty

Hitler's aggression

Weakness of League

Reasons for the outbreak of war.

Next stop Austria

Hitler was Austrian and longed to join the German-speaking country with Germany (although this was forbidden in the Treaty of Versailles).

In 1938 he instructed pro-German Austrians to start trouble in the country and then sent troops in to 'restore order'. The Austrian Chancellor resigned and Britain and France complained bitterly, but they were not prepared to take action. Britain preferred a policy of **appeasement** – preventing war by negotiation.

This policy was soon brought into action over Czechoslovakia. Hitler demanded that the Sudetenland area, where three million Germans lived, should be given to Germany. He threatened to invade if his wish was not granted. At a meeting in Munich in September 1938 Britain, France, Italy and Germany agreed that Germany should have the Sudetenland and Hitler said that he had no more land he wanted to gain. The British Prime Minister, Neville Chamberlain, was given a hero's reception when he returned to London. He had saved Europe from war. The Czechs were disgusted and President Benes resigned in protest.

Six months later Chamberlain realised that he had been tricked when Hitler invaded and occupied the rest of Czechoslovakia. Both Britain and France stepped up the process of arming themselves for the war that now seemed inevitable. Since Poland looked like Hitler's next target (it had been formed in 1919 partly with land taken from Germany) the two countries agreed to help Poland if Hitler attacked.

Britain and France did not expect Hitler to attack Poland because the Soviet Union also wanted land there and would not let Hitler occupy the country. But in August 1939 Stalin and Hitler decided that for the moment it suited them to be allies. They signed the Nazi-Soviet Pact and agreed to share Poland between them. On 1 September Hitler invaded and two days later Britain and France declared war – though there was little they could do to save Poland.

Things to do

'It was Hitler who caused the Second World War to break out in 1939. There was no other cause.' From what you have read on these pages, say whether or not you agree with this statement.

2.2 THE SECOND WORLD WAR

On 3 September 1939 Britain and Germany were again at war. Two days earlier German dive-bombers, low-flying fighter planes and armoured divisions smashed into Poland. This was Hitler's 'lightning war' or **blitzkrieg**. It worked against Poland and six months later Hitler struck again. Nazi troops overran Denmark, Norway, Holland and Belgium. On 12 May 1940, skirting round the old defences built since the war, German troops invaded France. The British Expeditionary Force, sent to help guard France's frontier with Belgium, was sliced in two. In the north, the BEF and French troops were trapped on the beach at Dunkirk. Hundreds of small boats, yachts and pleasure steamers heard about this and set out from Britain, and with the navy managed to rescue around 338,000 British and French soldiers from the beaches of Dunkirk. To the south, the Germans soon overran French forces, and on 22 June the French surrendered. From then until the end of the war, the Germans allowed the French to govern most of central and southern France from the town of Vichy, but the Vichy government was always under German control and influence.

After the fall of France, Britain stood alone against Nazi Germany and its allies (the Axis powers).

The war in Europe and North Africa, 1939–42.

Key:
- Neutral countries
- Axis powers and their allies
- Areas conquered by the Axis 1939–42 (with dates of conquest)
- Vichy France – ruled by the French under German influence

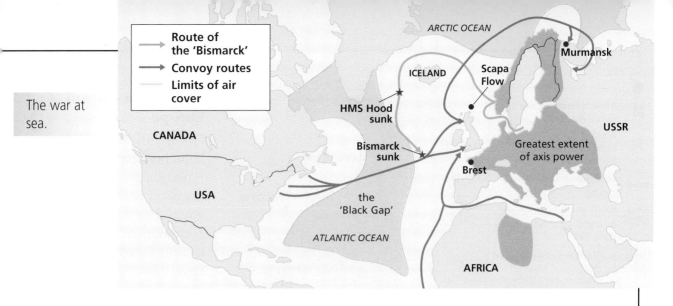

The war at sea.

The war at sea

Britain's survival as a nation and as a fighting force depended upon keeping the sea routes open. Along these sea routes, food and raw materials were shipped to Britain, and Britain was able to help supply the Allies. The aim of the Germans was to sink as many ships steaming for Britain as possible and so starve the British into surrender.

Allied cargo ships travelled in **convoys** with British destroyers to protect them from German attacks. Food, petrol and aeroplanes were shipped across the Atlantic from the USA and, after the USA joined in the war, troops crossed too. Arctic convoys carried lorries, tanks and aeroplanes to Russia. Supplies for the British Eighth Army were shipped through the Mediterranean Sea.

After the fall of France in 1940, German ships, based in the French port of Brest, attacked Allied shipping deep in the Atlantic. The German battleship *Bismarck* tried to get to Brest from the Baltic Sea to join them but, after sinking the British battleship *HMS Hood*, was itself sunk by the British navy.

German submarines (U-boats), operating from French ports, attacked convoys crossing the Atlantic. These U-boats hunted in packs and were so successful that Churchill, Britain's leader, talked about the 'Battle of the Atlantic'. In March 1943 forty U-boats attacked two Allied convoys, consisting of ninety-two ships, in the 'Black Gap' beyond the range of aircraft cover. One U-boat and twenty-one Allied ships were sunk.

The development of **sonar** meant that submarines could be detected quickly and accurately, and the breaking of German secret codes began to turn the war at sea in the Allies' favour.

Things to do

1 Look at the map 'The war in Europe and North Africa 1939–42'.
  a Make a list of the Axis powers and their allies.
  b Make a list of the countries conquered by the Axis powers, with dates.
  c Why do you think the Axis powers were able to overrun so much of Europe so quickly?

2 Now look at the map 'The war at sea'. Britain, an island, was fighting Germany, a land-based power.
  What were the advantages and disadvantages of
  a being an island at this time
  b being a land-based power at this time?

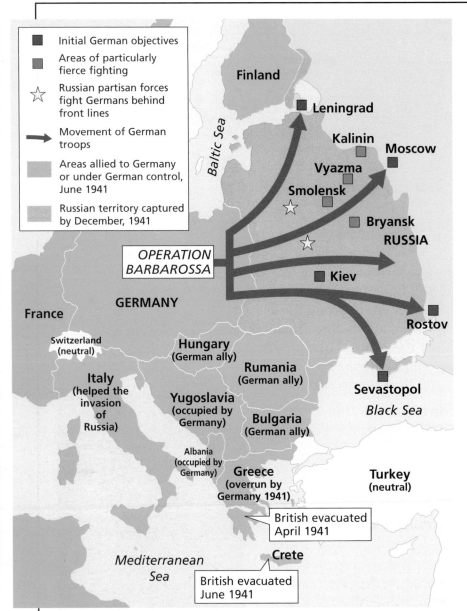

Legend:

- ■ Initial German objectives
- ■ Areas of particularly fierce fighting
- ☆ Russian partisan forces fight Germans behind front lines
- → Movement of German troops
- Areas allied to Germany or under German control, June 1941
- Russian territory captured by December, 1941

OPERATION BARBAROSSA

Finland

Baltic Sea

Leningrad
Kalinin
Moscow
Vyazma
Smolensk
Bryansk
RUSSIA
Kiev
Rostov

GERMANY

France

Switzerland (neutral)

Italy (helped the invasion of Russia)

Hungary (German ally)

Rumania (German ally)

Yugoslavia (occupied by Germany)

Bulgaria (German ally)

Albania (occupied by Germany)

Greece (overrun by Germany 1941)

British evacuated April 1941

Sevastopol

Black Sea

Turkey (neutral)

Crete

British evacuated June 1941

Mediterranean Sea

Operation Barbarossa.

The war in eastern Europe

On 22 June 1941 Hitler launched 'Operation Barbarossa'. This was the invasion of Russia. He wanted to defeat communism and he wanted to find *lebensraum* (living space) for the German people. This was probably Hitler's greatest mistake. In the end, campaigns over the vastness of Russia exhausted the German army.

At first the German 'blitzkrieg' was very successful and the Germans advanced deep into Russia. By the end of 1941 they had captured the Baltic countries and had laid siege to Leningrad (now called St Petersburg); they had reached the Black Sea, capturing the rich agricultural and industrial areas of the Ukraine on the way, and had reached the suburbs of Moscow.

What went wrong? German troops spent a terrible winter in Russia and it wasn't until June 1942 that they began to advance again. This time their aim was to capture Moscow and the oil-fields of the Caucasus. They were stopped at the city of Stalingrad (now called Volgograd). For five months the German army laid siege to the city. The Russians inside suffered dreadfully, and were reduced to eating stray cats and dogs as well as rats. Eventually Russian troops under their commander, Marshal Zhukov, surrounded the German army. In January 1943, 100,000 soldiers and 23 generals surrendered.

The Russians pushed the Germans back and back until, by the end of 1944, all Russian lands had been recaptured and the Russian armies were invading Germany.

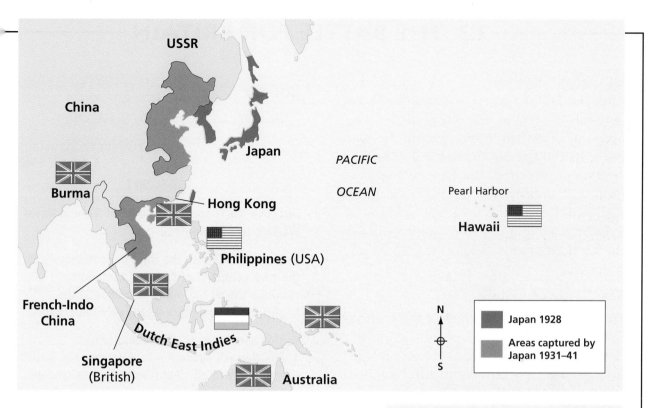

USSR
China
Japan
PACIFIC
OCEAN
Burma
Hong Kong
Pearl Harbor
Hawaii
Philippines (USA)
French-Indo
China
Dutch East Indies
Singapore
(British)
Australia

N
S

Japan 1928

Areas captured by
Japan 1931–41

The expansion of Japan.

The war in the Far East 1931–42

Japan was trying to create an empire in the Far East long before the Second World War broke out. By the beginning of 1941 the Japanese controlled large areas of eastern China. This was part of their plan, called the Greater East Asia Co-prosperity Sphere, by which they aimed to gain economic control of the Far East. But in their way stood the British Empire and the US navy.

In 1940, when Britain stood alone against Nazi Germany, the British Empire seemed to be collapsing. Certainly Great Britain, fighting for survival, was not able to send troops to defend Singapore or Burma. The USA was a different matter. Strong, and keeping out of the war, America greatly disapproved of Japan's military expansion, and might use its huge fleet, stationed in the Pacific at Pearl Harbor in the Hawaiian Islands, to oppose it. And Hitler had guaranteed to support Japan in the event of an Allied attack. Japan took a chance. Without warning, on Sunday 7 December 1941, 400 Japanese planes rained bombs and torpedoes onto the American fleet. They sank or severely damaged 18 warships and killed nearly 3000 people. Japan had entered the Second World War. But so, too, had America.

Things to do

1 Operation Barbarossa failed for more than one reason. It failed because of:
  - the terrible Russian winter
  - long supply lines: German troops were a long way from a friendly country willing to supply them with food and materials
  - the Russian 'scorched earth' policy – retreating Russian soldiers burned everything they left behind, so the Germans could not use it
  - the Russian success at Stalingrad.
  Put these reasons in order of importance, explaining why you have chosen that particular order.

2 a Why did Japan bomb Pearl Harbor?
  b What risks were the Japanese government taking in doing so?
  c Did the risks pay off?

Operation Sealion

After the fall of France, Hitler ordered his generals in 1941 to prepare plans for an invasion of Britain. At French and Belgian ports 100,000 troops assembled. Landing craft were prepared. But there was no point in a cross-channel invasion if the RAF could bomb the invading fleet out of existence. Germany had to gain control of the air if Operation Sealion was to be a success.

The Battle of Britain

Herman Goering, the chief of the German Luftwaffe (airforce) was given the job of destroying the RAF. It looked as if it was going to be easy. The Luftwaffe had 2670 planes and the RAF 600. The Luftwaffe, however, had more bombers than fighters, and their fighters could only operate for half an hour at a time, before they ran out of fuel. The RAF also had **radar**, which could pin-point the position of enemy planes and direct fighter squadrons accurately. The battle was not going to be easy.

On 15 August 1940 the Luftwaffe began an all-out effort to smash the RAF. For nearly a month the skies of southern England were filled with the vapour trails of battling aircraft. Airfields were bombed and hundreds of fighters shot down. By the beginning of September the RAF was dangerously short of planes and pilots. It was reckoned that the life expectancy of an RAF fighter pilot was just fourteen days.

Suddenly it stopped. German High Command had decided the Luftwaffe's losses were too great. The Luftwaffe turned to bombing Britain's cities and Hitler decided to try to invade Russia. Operation Sealion was called off.

Source A

The orders sent by Hitler to the Luftwaffe.

Führer's Headquarters
1 August 1940

TOP SECRET

Directive No.17 for the Conduct of Air and Naval Warfare against England.

In order to establish the conditions necessary for the final conquest of England, I intend to continue the air and naval war against the English homeland more intensively than before.

To this end I issue the following orders:
1 The German airforce is to overcome the British airforce with all means at its disposal and as soon as possible.
2 Attacks on the harbours of the south coast are to be undertaken on the smallest scale possible, in view of our intended operations.
3 The Luftwaffe is to stand by in force for Operation Sealion.

ADOLF HITLER

All RAF pilots were men, but women also played their part in the Battle of Britain. In this painting a WAAF (Women's Auxiliary Airforce) squad is raising a barrage balloon outside Coventry. Barrage balloons were attached to the ground by cables. If an enemy plane flew too low, it either hit the balloon or got entangled in the cables.

Source B

Source C

An account of the first day of the Blitz in Stepney, in the East End of London – one of many reports collected by 'Mass Observation'.

At 8.15 p.m. a colossal crash, as if the whole street was collapsing; the shelter itself is shaking. Immediately an ARP (Air Raid Precaution) helper, a nurse, begins singing lustily in an attempt to drown out the noise: 'Roll out the barrel' while Mrs S., wife of a dyer and cleaner, screams 'My house! It hit my house! My house is blown to bits!' As the bombing continues, a man shouts at the ARP helper who is still trying to get people to sing, 'Shut your bleedin' row!'

The Blitz

Once Hitler realised that he could not defeat the RAF, he tried to bomb the British into submission in the Blitz. From September 1940 to May 1941 bombs rained down on London and other major cities. Although London was the main target, ports and harbours, factories and homes throughout Britain were destroyed. This put tremendous pressure on the rescue, fire-fighting and ambulance services. Communal air-raid shelters were built at the end of streets; people had Anderson air-raid shelters, which were corrugated steel huts covered with earth, in their gardens. They had Morrison shelters, which were steel tables, inside their houses. Thousands of Londoners slept on Underground railway platforms. At night, people volunteered to 'fire watch'; street lights and car headlights were dimmed and every window had 'black-out' curtains, pulled so that not a chink of light could show. This 'black-out' made it difficult for German bombers to spot their targets. Sirens wailed when a raid was about to start so that people could take shelter.

Even so, by the end of May 1941, over 60,000 British people had been killed. Then Hitler turned his attention to Russia.

This photograph was taken in London during the Blitz.

Things to do

1 Read Source A.
   a What did Hitler plan to do?
   b Why did he fail?

2 Make a list of the ways people tried to protect themselves from the bombs. Which do you think would have been the most effective?

3 How helpful is Source C in telling you what the Blitz was like?

4 Look carefully at Source D. Many people believe this was a posed photograph to be used for propaganda.
   a What clues can you find which might suggest the photo was posed?
   b How, and by whom, could the photo be used for propaganda purposes?

2.4 BOMBS, BOMBS, BOMBS

Why bomb?

Allied and Axis planes bombed cities. They bombed to destroy factories and docks, shipyards and railways. They bombed to create fear in ordinary people and destroy morale.

Precision bombing

Some raids were made on military targets like factories and shipyards. In 1943 Allied planes made a daring raid on the German rocket factory at Peenemunde. In the same year 'bouncing bombs', developed by Barnes Wallis, were used to damage the Mohne and Eder dams in the Ruhr.

However, it was difficult to hit targets accurately. Night flying was difficult unless there was a moon. Even then, cloud and smoke tended to blot out the targets, and fighter planes, barrage balloons, searchlights and anti-aircraft guns made the job even more difficult. It was easier to bomb in daylight – but it was easier for the fighters, too, to locate and bring down the bombers before they reached their targets. Before long, precision bombing was virtually abandoned. Airforce leaders began to think that, in total war, no distinction should be made between armed forces and civilians.

Source B

Bombs dropped on Britain and Germany 1940–5.

Year	Britain	Germany
1940	37,000	10,000
1941	21,000	30,000
1942	3000	40,000
1943	9000	120,000
1944	2000	650,000
1945	750	500,000

Source C

Written by Vera Brittain in 1943.

The change from the 'precision' bombing of military objectives to the present 'obliteration' bombing of whole areas with their churches, libraries, schools, hospitals, museums and vulnerable human beings came with the appointment of Sir Arthur Harris to the control of Bomber Command on 3 March 1942.

This is a policy of murder and massacre in the name of the British people.

Source A

"By the way, did you remember to feed the canary?"

This cartoon was published during the Second World War.

Dresden 1945: necessity or revenge?

By the beginning of 1945 it was clear that the Allies would win the war. It was only a matter of time. In order to bring the war in Europe to a quick end, the Allies decided on 'Operation Thunderclap': a massive assault on civilian targets planned to break the morale of ordinary German people. The target chosen was Dresden, a beautiful medieval city that had never been bombed before. On the nights of 13 and 14 February the RAF and USAAF destroyed the city. Over 135,000 people died in a horrific firestorm, a far greater number than the 51,500 British civilians killed by the Luftwaffe during the whole of the war.

Dresden after the Allied raids of 1945.

Source D

Source E

Sir Arthur Harris, who was in charge of Bomber Command 1942–5, explains why he ordered the bombing of Dresden.

Dresden had by this time become the main centre of communications for the defence of Germany. It was also by far the largest city in Germany which had been left intact; it had never been bombed. As a large centre of war industry it was also of the highest importance.

Source F

From a radio broadcast by the official German foreign information services.

The Americans have proved that they can hit precise targets whenever they please. It would therefore have been possible to have spared the residential districts of Dresden and the historic town centre. The use of incendiaries (fire bombs) proves that residential districts were being deliberately attacked. It is pointless to drop incendiaries on railways.

Things to do

1 a What was the difference between precision bombing and mass bombing?
  b Why was the switch made to mass bombing?

2 Look at Source A.
  a What point is the cartoonist trying to make?
  b Mass bombing was supposed to break people's morale. Does this cartoon prove that it didn't?

3 Look at Source B.
  What do the figures tell you about:
  a Allied air power
  b the damage done to Germany during the war?

4 a Make a list, using the sources and information in this unit, of all the reasons there were for bombing Dresden.
  b Which of these do you think was the most important at the time?
  c Why do you think the Allies bombed Dresden? Remember to back up what you say with evidence from this unit.

5 Can there ever be good reasons for bombing civilians?

2.5 KEEPING THE CHILDREN SAFE?

What was evacuation?

The British government made plans to send children from cities to live in the countryside where they would be safe. In London, the plans were put into operation on 1 September 1939 and within four days over one million children were sent to the West Country and to Wales. But because the bombs didn't fall immediately, parents gradually took their children back home. There was another wave of evacuation in 1940 when the Blitz began, and again in 1944 when Germany began launching the V1 and V2 'flying bombs'.

How did evacuation work?

Mothers usually went with children under school age, but most children went alone or with their brothers and sisters. Sometimes teachers would go with the children in their class. The children had a label tied on them giving their name and home address. They could take one suitcase and had to have their gas mask with them. Parents did not always know where their children were going when they set off. They just had to believe government promises that their children would be well looked after.

The children were **billeted** with families who had room for them. The government paid families 10s 6d a week for the first child billeted and 8s 6d a week each for any others. Not all the families wanted children from the big cities staying with them, and not all the children wanted to live away from home. Some children settled in well, others were desperately unhappy.

Source A

Children walking to Blackhouse Road station, north-east London, in 1939 to be evacuated.

Source B

Beryl Hewitson describes what happened to her when she arrived in the country.

We were told to sit quietly on the floor while villagers and farmers' wives came to choose which children they wanted. Eventually only my friend Nancy and myself were left – two plain, straight-haired little girls wearing glasses, now rather tearful. A large, happy-looking, middle-aged lady rushed in asking, 'Is that all you have left?' A sad, slow nod of the head from our teacher. 'I'll take the poor bairns.' We were led out of the hall with this stranger and taken to a farm where we spent two years.

Source C

Patricia Barton remembers life as an evacuee.

The village didn't know what hit them when we first arrived. It was gang warfare between us and the local kids. There wasn't a fruit tree within miles around with a single item of fruit left on it. After a while things settled down to an uneasy truce.

Source D

Extracts from reports sent to the Women's Institute Headquarters in 1940.

The children were filthy; we have never seen so many children with lice and nits lacking any knowledge of clean and hygienic habits. It seemed they hadn't bathed for months; some children had dirty, septic sores all over their bodies. Some of the children were sewn into their ragged little garments. There was hardly a child with a whole pair of shoes. Many of the mothers and children were bedwetters and were not in the habit of doing anything else.

Source E

Chris Portinari had three homes as an evacuee. He was sent away from the first because he helped himself to sugar. Two boys in the second home bullied him very badly.

They would tie me to a chair and held red-hot pokers in front of my eyes. I had terrible nightmares. I was sent away when the three of us took down the knickers of the girl next door. I ended up in a spick and span place. Every day I would come home from school to 'Clean this, shine that.' So I started to save my milk money, a halfpenny a day. I came home one day and wrote across the list of things to do, 'GONE BACK TO LONDON'. My mother hid me in the attic for two days before telling my father. I wasn't sent back and stayed in London during the raids.

Source F

Some women looked after many evacuee children! They could be awarded the British Empire Medal for doing this.

Source G

Sheila Price was the second of eight children from Hammersmith, London. She was evacuated when she was twelve years old.

The orchard bore fruit, we had a car to take us to school, a piano, a beautiful home, servants, typing lessons, mini-golf and a fine lawn. Most of all we met warmth and understanding.

I became a snob. Each weekend I'd board the bus home. The street looked dingy, poor – I hated it. I remember seeing my father cooking a pigeon on our kitchen fire and the repulsion stayed with me. Eventually Mother called me home to look after the others. Then my lovely world crumbled.

Things to do

1 Design a poster to encourage parents to send their children away from the cities.

2 Look at Source A.
These children are being sent away from their parents to live with strangers for an indefinite length of time.
Why do you think everyone seems to be smiling and cheerful?

3 Read Source B.
Here villagers chose the children they wanted. Do you think this was the right way of deciding which children should go with which adults? Can you work out a better system? Remember this was wartime and decisions had to be made quickly.

4 a Make a list of the problems faced by:
  - evacuees
  - the families with whom they lived.
b 'There would have been no problems if the evacuee children had tried harder to fit in with their new families'. Explain whether you would agree or disagree with this statement.

5 Why did evacuee children have such different experiences?

2.6 WINNIE'S WAR

Winnie Farley married Leslie Williams in 1938. War was declared the following year, and Leslie volunteered to fight. He joined the Royal Engineers and in February 1941 was sent abroad to Africa and then the Middle East. Five months later, Winnie and Leslie's daughter Margaret was born. Leslie didn't see her until she was four years old.

Here Winnie remembers her war.

Keeping in touch

I never really knew where Leslie was. We wives weren't supposed to, but sometimes he would be able to write that he had had some leave in Alexandria, or Gaza, so I knew he was still in the Middle East. I sent him parcels. He always wanted Keatings Powders to kill the lice and bed bugs. I knitted mittens and socks and woollen caps. When I could get eggs and fat I baked cakes for him and sent them out in tins. He always wanted soap, too, especially shaving soap. Everything took such a long time. It was three weeks before he got the news that Margaret had been born.

A photograph of Leslie, taken during the war.

War work

Before Margaret was born I worked in Chichester as a nurse with the VADs [Voluntary Aid Detachment]. I nursed soldiers and civilians. In 1940, after Dunkirk, we all thought Hitler was going to invade and the south coast was a dangerous place to be. The civilian patients were all taken somewhere safer and we were left with the soldiers. For some reason I wasn't thought good enough to nurse soldiers so I was sent to nurse people who were mentally disturbed. Every door had to be locked and unlocked. As well as having a huge bunch of keys, I also carried a whistle which I had to blow if there was trouble. I'll always remember Georgie. She would go to sleep sitting bolt upright and with her eyes wide open. She pushed a wicker chair everywhere she went, even to the loo.

Air raids and eiderdowns

When I was at home in Chichester and the sirens went, I would take the baby into bed with me and pull the eiderdown over both of us. An ATS officer was billeted with us and she used to come under the eiderdown too! She said she wasn't afraid – she just couldn't stop shaking.

Fish and blackcurrants

Fish wasn't rationed, but there wasn't much of it. I queued for hours for a piece of plaice for Margaret. And then she would only eat it if it was covered with blackcurrant purée. What a waste of good fish! And I had queued for so long for it!

Air raids and shelters

We had a Sussex spaniel called Nobby who came with us when we visited my parents in Croydon. If there was an air raid, he rushed out of the house and was waiting by the shelter door almost before the sirens had stopped. He was always the first out of the shelter when the 'All clear' sounded.

Butter

Butter was rationed – sometimes to only 2oz a week. I used to pour the top of the milk into a small jar and screwed the top on tightly. Then I shook and shook the jar until the milk turned to butter.

Children's parties

My friend Joan was upset because she hadn't any eggs and so couldn't make a cake for Paul's third birthday. So I made it for her, and instead of eggs I used liquid paraffin. It worked beautifully: the cake rose well and was very tasty.

A woman we knew asked us to bring our children to a party. You never saw such food! There were scones thick with butter, iced cakes and chocolate biscuits. She must have got it all on the **black market**. *We always wondered what she did to get it!*

Sausages and ham

We were only allowed 4oz [113 grams] *of meat a week, but sausages, when you could get them, weren't rationed. Our butcher sold sausage 'sandwiches'. He put a slice of sausage meat in between two slices of potato and dipped the whole thing in dried milk and breadcrumbs. They were really quite tasty. Sometimes I managed to get a ham knuckle with a bit of meat left on it. I shaved off the bits of ham and cooked them with potatoes and herbs. The ham bone I boiled up with split peas to make a good soup.*

Eggs and hens

Eggs were rationed to one a week and sometimes one every two weeks. An old lady in the next village kept hens and used to let me have eggs for Margaret. Then the men from the ministry caught up with her and she had to stop. So she gave me two hens which she said had stopped laying. But they laid two eggs a day for me all through the war, except on Sundays when they only managed one.

A photograph of Winnie and Margaret, taken during the war.

Source B

Things to do

1 Why was it so difficult to keep in touch with men fighting overseas?

2 a Why was food rationed during the war?

  b Do you think people would have been less or more healthy as a result?

3 What words do you think Winnie would have used to describe her war? *Frightening? Fun? Worrying? Lonely? Boring?* Explain your answer, using all the information on these two pages.

2.7 THE SECRET ARMIES: THE RESISTANCE MOVEMENTS IN OCCUPIED EUROPE

By 1942 Hitler controlled most of Europe. (Look back at the map on page 128 to remind yourself of which these countries were.) Each country became a **police state**, with a governor and an army of occupation. People living in these countries had a difficult choice. They could **collaborate** with the enemy. They could join a resistance movement, which was dangerous because if they were caught they could expect no mercy. Or they could try to get on with their lives as best they could. This was what most people did. But in every occupied country there were people resisting the enemy occupiers.

The French Resistance

One of the most famous resistance groups was the French Maquis. School children and milkmen, mayors and plumbers, café owners and teachers all tried in their own ways to undermine the German occupation.

The French Maquis hid Allied airmen who had been shot down and organised escape routes for them. They blew up bridges and railway lines. They made contact with the Free French forces in exile in Britain and their leader, Charles de Gaulle.

The Germans wreaked terrible revenge on any Maquis they caught. They destroyed the village of Oradour-sur-Glane and killed all the men, women and children living there because of the activities of local resistance groups. Later they discovered they had got the wrong village. By 1944 the Maquis were openly fighting the Germans and sending intelligence reports to Britain to help with the D-Day landings.

Source A

From a book called *Maquis* by G. Millar published in 1945.

For supplies we relied on Paincheau. We needed petrol. The Germans kept it in tanks in a guarded building. One night they parked a tanker beside a wall of the building that was not guarded. One man, a stonemason, silently cut a hole in the wall. His comrades ran a pipe through to the tank and all night pumped out petrol. The mason then rebuilt the wall. They did the same thing the next night. Finally, before the Germans noticed the levels going down, Paincheau's men put 200 kilos of sugar in the tank. [Sugar dissolves in petrol, so the Germans would not know it was there until they filled their vehicles with the petrol. The sugar in the petrol would then ruin the engines.]

Source B

In this photograph Danish resistance workers from Odense listen to a radio broadcast from London in 1945. If they had been caught, the Nazis would have killed them. The BBC broadcast coded instructions to resistance workers; it broadcast news of the war, which was different from the Nazi version; and it broadcast the first bars from Beethoven's 5th symphony. Listen to them. They sound just like the Morse Code for 'V' (which is dot, dot, dot, dash). V for victory, of course.

The Netherlands

The Resistance flourished in the Netherlands, in spite of Seyss-Inquart, the Reichskommissar for the Netherlands. He was hated by the Dutch because of his brutal regime. The Dutch Resistance ran underground newspapers which spread information. German offices were blown up and leading Nazis were assassinated. Although the Nazis sent 5 million Dutch workers to Germany, the Resistance hid 300,000 runaways and gave them false papers. Many families hid Jews to prevent their deportation. Even so, around 104,000 out of 140,000 Dutch Jews died in Nazi concentration camps.

Source C

In 1942 Anne Frank, her parents and sister Margot, together with four other Jews, went into hiding in a secret annexe in Otto Frank's office. Loyal friends kept them supplied and kept them safe. Anne kept a diary.

11 July 1942 We've forbidden Margot to cough even though she has a bad cold, and are giving her large doses of codeine.

24 December 1943 Whenever someone comes in from outside, with the wind in their clothes and the cold on their cheeks, I feel like burying my head under the blankets to keep from thinking 'When will we be allowed to breathe fresh air again?'

3 April 1944 The high point is our weekly slice of liver sausage, and jam on our unbuttered bread. But we're still alive!

21 July 1944 I'm finally getting optimistic. Now, at last, things are going well! They really are! Great news! An assassination attempt has been made on Hitler's life. The prospect of going back to school in October is making me too happy!

Someone tipped off the Gestapo. On 4 August 1944 they arrested Anne and her family. Her mother died of hunger and exhaustion in the Auschwitz concentration camp on 6 January 1945. Margot and Anne were moved from Auschwitz to the Bergen-Belsen concentration camp. There they died from typhus sometime in February or March 1945. The Allies liberated Belsen on 12 April 1945. Their father, Otto, survived until 1980.

Source D

Large resistance groups operated in Nazi-occupied parts of the Soviet Union. They formed partisan armies – armed civilians who fought occupying troops. These Russians are being hanged by the Germans because they were partisans.

Things to do

1 Most people in occupied Europe just tried to get on with their lives as best they could. What reasons might some have had for joining resistance movements?

2 Read Source A.
Was this really an important act of sabotage? Why would the Maquis risk death just for stealing some petrol?

3 Read Source C.
Why would some people risk everything to keep Jews like the Frank family alive? Why were others prepared to betray them?

4 Look at Sources B and D.
   a Why did the Nazis punish resistance fighters so severely?
   b Why was listening to the radio so important that people would risk their lives to do it?

The British realised that resistance groups in occupied Europe were helping to sabotage the German war effort and could supply the Allies with useful information. In July 1940 Winston Churchill, Britain's Prime Minister, set up the Special Operations Executive (SOE) to, as he said, *co-ordinate all action by way of* **subversion** *and sabotage against the enemy overseas.* France had fallen and Britain was, then, the only European country to stand against Nazi Germany. The RAF, after the Battle of Britain and the Blitz, was too weak for an immediate air strike on Germany. So Britain sent small raiding parties along the coasts of Europe and parachuted secret agents behind enemy lines. These secret agents worked with, and sometimes helped to set up, local resistance groups.

SOE agents went to the Balkans, the Baltic, Italy, Scandinavia, the Netherlands, Belgium, France and central Europe. Their success depended largely on local politics and geography. They could not, for example, stop the Nazis penetrating the Dutch Resistance, which led to the deaths of over 20,000 people. On the other hand, the SOE worked successfully with Yugoslavian partisans fighting German troops in the mountains. However, most SOE agents worked in France, where almost 200 of them were executed. In 1945 only 30 agents survived.

Source A

This canister is going to be dropped behind enemy lines in France. It contains equipment for the Maquis.

Source B

Major-General Sir Colin Gubbins, Head of the SOE.

All contacts with occupied countries closed when the last British forces returned to Great Britain in 1940, so the first man to go back to any country had to be parachuted 'blind'. There was no one waiting to receive him on the dropping ground, no household ready to give him shelter, conceal his kit and arrange his onward passage.

Source C

An aircraft carrying SOE agents drops SOE equipment for agents on the ground.

VIOLETTE SZABO

Violette's father was an English soldier who met and married her mother in France at the end of the First World War. Violette spent her childhood in Brixton, London and worked in Woolworth's when she left school. She married a Free French soldier and because she spoke fluent French worked for the SOE. She was parachuted into France many times and in the 1950s her story was made into a film *Carve Her Name with Pride*. This is the story of her last mission.

It was just before D-Day and Violette was parachuted into France to take charge of a Maquis unit. Things went badly wrong. Violette and the local Maquis leader were ambushed by an SS Unit trying to get to Normandy and the D-Day beaches. Injured, Violette urged the Maquis leader to get away. He had more important things to do than save her life. She took cover behind some trees in a cornfield and for two hours held off 400 Germans and two tanks. Finally she ran out of ammunition and was captured. The Maquis planned her rescue but she was moved unexpectedly to Paris. Then, in August 1944 Violette was sent to Ravensbruck, an enormous concentration camp for women. There, on 26 January 1945, when the Allies were invading Germany and the war in France was over, she was condemned to death, shot in the neck from behind, and cremated.

HARRY RÉE (HENRI)

Harry Rée was a graduate of Cambridge University and a school teacher when he joined the SOE. He parachuted into France many times, set up and ran resistance networks, killed and sabotaged. He was never caught. This is the story of one of his exploits.

Captain Harry Rée.

The great Peugeot car works at Sochaux was making gun-carriers and gun turrets for German Panzers. The RAF had not been able to do more than damage it. Harry was asked to destroy the works from inside, by sabotage. Monsieur Sire, the personnel manager at the works, secretly supported the Resistance. He gave Harry a pass and arranged for him to see Rudolphe Peugeot, the boss. Monsieur Peugeot gave Harry the factory plans. He helped him select the points where the explosives should be placed and introduced him to two trustworthy factory foremen. Harry arranged for explosives to be smuggled inside the factory and hidden in a cleaner's cupboard. On the chosen night, the foremen, avoiding the sentries, placed the charges in the transformer hall, the assembly plant and the steel presses and escaped through the nightwatchman's room. At ten minutes past midnight the works blew up. Within minutes SS and army units arrived and cordoned off the whole area. The next morning Sochaux was swarming with the dreaded Gestapo. No one was caught.

Things to do

1 Why was the SOE set up?

2 a If you were a recruiting officer for the SOE, what sort of person would you select?
  b What training do you think SOE agents should have had?

3 What problems did SOE agents face when they were parachuted into occupied Europe? Use Source B and any other information in this unit in your answer.

4 Look at Sources A and C. What dangers and difficulties faced members of the Resistance:
  a in receiving an RAF 'drop'
  b in working with SOE agents behind enemy lines?

5 Use the story of either Violette Szabo or Harry Rée to write your own story about the SOE and the French Resistance.

What was it like to live in occupied Europe?

Most people in occupied Europe tried to get on with their everyday lives as best they could. But what was life like for them?

The economies of these countries were adjusted to serve the needs of Germany. Firms were taken over and raw materials and fuel used for German projects. Thousands of workers were sent to Germany to help with the German war effort. Banks were also taken over and German gold reserves grew. Everything cost more.

Source A

The woman with the shaved head was said to have had her baby by a German soldier. Now, carrying her baby, she is jeered and shouted at by the people where she lives. This photograph was taken in 1945 after the Germans had left France.

There were hundreds of everyday reminders of the Nazi take-over. German soldiers patrolled the streets, ate and drank in the cafés and bars. They took what they wanted, whether it was art treasures or girlfriends.

Some people decided they could survive best by working with the Nazi invaders. At the end of the war they paid a terrible price for this collaboration.

VIDKUN QUISLING (1887–1945)

Quisling was a Norwegian diplomat. In the 1920s he worked for the League of Nations. From 1931 to 1933 he was Defence Minister in Norway. In 1933, when Hitler came to power in Germany, he founded the *Nasjonal Samlung* (National Party) which was really an imitation of Hitler's Nazi Party. In April 1940 the German army and airforce began a massive assault on Norway. King Haakon and his government tried desperately to organise resistance. However, the Norwegian army was no match for the highly organised, efficient German war machine and, despite support from the RAF and the Royal Navy, Norway surrendered. The King and his government fled to Britain where they formed a Norwegian government-in-exile.

Vidkun Quisling stayed in Norway. The Nazis banned all political parties except the *Nasjonal Samlung* and Quisling became Prime Minister. He ran Norway just as the Nazis wanted, which was not, of course, how the Norwegian government-in-exile wanted things done. When Norway was liberated in May 1945, Quisling gave himself up to the Norwegian police. Evidence was produced at his trial which proved he was in regular and secret contact with the Nazis before the war, urging them to invade Norway. He was found guilty of high treason and shot by a firing squad.

His treachery was thought to be so dreadful that the word 'quisling' has come to mean 'traitor'.

WILLIAM JOYCE (1906–46)

Britain's most famous traitor was William Joyce. Born in New York, he had Irish parents who took him to Ireland, where they lived until he was sixteen. In 1922 they emigrated to England and William Joyce joined the British Union of Fascists. He fled to Germany before war broke out. Between September 1939 and April 1945, Joyce broadcast to the British people from *Radio Hamburg*. His broadcasts were streams of propaganda and hatred. He told of villages and towns that would be bombed, of ships that would be sunk and of invasion plans. He also needled the British about food prices and censorship. British people became used to turning on their radios and hearing his posh voice saying 'Germany calling; Germany calling', and nicknamed him 'Lord Haw-Haw'. Eventually most people learned to laugh at him, but they still worried that what he said might be right. British troops captured Joyce near the Danish/German frontier and brought him back to Britain. Accused of treason, he was found guilty at the Old Bailey and later hanged.

HENRI PHILIPPE PÉTAIN (1856–1951)

Pétain was a French soldier and politician. When he was a junior officer his confidential report said 'If this officer rises above the rank of major, it will be a disaster for France.' By 1917 he was Commander-in-Chief of the French army and revered as a war hero and saviour of his country.

Pétain was 84 when German troops began their advance through Belgium in 1939. The French government asked him to join them because it needed his advice. He said the government should not consider a military alliance with Great Britain. Once Germany had invaded France and occupied Paris, Pétain said that the French government should not carry on fighting, but should ask for an **armistice**. The Germans divided France into two zones: the north (occupied) and the south (unoccupied). Pétain led the government of the unoccupied south of France from the city of Vichy. He ran unoccupied France as the Germans wanted him to. The only thing he refused to do was to allow France to fight Britain. He dreamed of a state based on 'work, family and fatherland', which was very close to the Nazi idea of what a state should be. He abolished trade unions, set up official state youth organisations and allowed only one political party. Vichy France had an anti-Jewish policy and was nothing like the sort of France for which the Free French were fighting. Pétain was arrested when the Allies liberated France in 1944. He was accused of treason, tried and found guilty. Because of his age he was not executed but sentenced to life imprisonment.

Things to do

1 a What is the difference between a collaborator and a traitor?
  b Why might some people have become collaborators?

2 Look at Source A.
  a How is this woman being punished?
  b Why do you think she was not brought to a court of law like Pétain, Quisling and Joyce?

3 Read about William Joyce (Lord Haw-Haw). Why did the British authorities take such a serious view of what he did?

4 Quisling and Pétain both ran their countries when they were occupied by Germans. What are the similarities and what are the differences between what they did?

At the end of the war they were both accused of being traitors. In your judgement, were Pétain, Quisling and Joyce traitors? Explain your answer.

All countries need spies in wartime to tell them of enemy plans for battles. All countries need to keep secrets, too. War Offices need to send orders to army, navy and airforce commanders without the enemy listening to them.

Governments do not always tell the truth to their own people about the way the war is going. They need to keep their people at home believing that all is going well: that the war will be won.

Source B

You never know who's listening!

CARELESS TAL
COSTS LIVES

In Britain a whole series of posters warned people about the dangers of gossiping.

Source A

This photograph shows rescue workers searching for survivors in a bombed-out school. It is dated 20 January 1943 and was marked 'banned'.

Source C

This poster was designed to make people see that what they may regard as a nuisance (petrol going up in price) was nothing compared to the hardships suffered by merchant seamen. It was very nearly banned because the censor thought it would discourage men from joining the navy.

"The price of petrol has been increased by one penny" – Official

The Enigma machine

Commanders usually communicated with their troops by radio. The problem was that they could never be sure whether or not the enemy was listening in. The Germans solved the problem by inventing the 'Enigma' machine. This 'scrambled' straightforward messages into code which no one could understand unless they had an up-to-date code book. To make things even more difficult, Enigma was automatically adjusted minute by minute. The British government set up a 'Codes and Cyphers School' at Bletchley Park in Buckinghamshire. Details about Enigma were passed on to the British by a Polish worker in the factory where they were made. Eventually the Enigma code was broken, but the British government kept this a secret. They let the Germans believe they were still trying – and listened in to all the messages sent via Enigma.

The man who never was

In 1943 British Intelligence dressed a dead man in a Royal Marine's uniform and put false papers in his pockets. They chained a briefcase full of invasion plans to his wrist. Then they floated him in the sea off the coast of Spain. When the body was washed ashore, German agents quickly got hold of the papers in the man's briefcase. They were detailed invasion plans – but for the south coast of France, not the Normandy beaches where the Allies really planned to stage their come-back in Europe.

Source D

An Enigma machine.

RUDOLF ROSSLER

Rudolf Rossler was one of the most successful spies of the Second World War. He was a German and in 1933, when Hitler came to power, Rossler went to live in Lucerne, Switzerland. There he joined a Russian spy-ring and was given the code-name 'Lucy'.

Rossler kept in contact with his friends in Germany. Many of them became high-ranking officers in the army and navy and influential Nazis. Without realising it, they gave him a lot of highly secret information. He was able to tell the Allies about Germany's plans to attack Poland, Denmark and Norway; he warned the Russians about Operation Barbarossa and about German preparations for an attack on the Russians at Kursk in 1943.

The 'Lucy Ring' was never broken and was one of the best wartime spy rings.

Things to do

1 Look at Source A.
  Why do you think the government would not allow this photograph to be published?

2 Look at Source B.
  a Hitler and Goering would never really have sat behind these women on the top of a bus! Why, then, did the artist draw them there?
  b Design your own war-time poster. What point do you want to make?

3 The government nearly banned the poster in Source C.
  a What point was the artist trying to make?
  b Do you think he made his point successfully?

4 How would you have gone about setting up a spy-ring in occupied Europe?

Over here!

On 26 January 1942 American troops began to arrive in Britain. By May 1944 there were 1,526,965 American soldiers, sailors and airmen stationed in the UK, ready to take part in an Allied invasion of Hitler's Europe. These troops (called GIs because their uniform was supposed to be stamped 'General Issue') were well-fed, well-dressed and well-paid, and they had a huge impact on the British people with whom they came into contact.

The USAAF

By far the biggest impact was made by the USAAF (United States Army Air Forces) who were stationed throughout Britain and who became involved with local people in the towns and villages near to their bases. Although most GIs were stationed in East Anglia, there were many elsewhere in England and in Wales, Scotland and Northern Ireland.

Non-combat troops

As well as combat troops, there were GIs who were responsible for supplying vehicles and planes, uniforms, food, guns,

Source A

Source B

A woman who was a teenager during the Second World War remembers:

Americans were 'cheeky' compared to our usual 'Mr Frigidaire Englishman', but what a boost to her ego when one is greeted with 'Hello Duchess!' (and you were treated like one!) or 'Hi, beautiful!' That was so GOOD! As we got to know these boys, how generous they were; we never lacked for chocolates or cigarettes or even precious luxuries like nylons that they could get for us.

tanks, ammunition and everything a fighting force needed in order to operate efficiently. This sort of back-up is called 'supply and maintenance'.

Marrying local girls

The two major US supply bases were in the north-west of England, at Burtonwood and Warton in Lancashire, which together housed 33,000 men by 1945. These men stayed on the same base all the time and had time off in nearby towns like Preston, Manchester and Liverpool. From Burtonwood alone, 7000 men married local girls between 1942 and 1993 when the base closed. During the Second World War there were 75,000 GI brides in Britain – and most of them eventually left their family and friends and went to join their new husbands in the USA.

Apart from this very obvious impact, the American GIs affected British people's language, their music and their general idea of how to have fun.

Children stop an American GI to ask 'Have you any gum, chum?' They often did and gave it away freely. Sometimes the chewing gum became a currency, to be paid for going on errands to buy fish and chips or to fix a date with a boy's sister.

Source C

A GI from Virginia remembers being invited home by a girl he met at a dance:

We had a meal which even by American standards was great – complete with ham and much more. Only afterwards did I discover that I had eaten the family's rations for a month. So I soon corrected that. I went to see our Mess Sergeant and the next time I turned up at this girl's home, it was as if I was Santa Claus. I brought a large can of pears and a pork loin – and a lot more stuff.

British families were encouraged to entertain GIs. It was soon ruled that GIs should take special rations with them for each day's stay: fruit or tomato juice, evaporated milk, peas, bacon, sugar, coffee, lard, butter and rice.

GI wives and babies wave goodbye to England from SS *Argentina*, one of the first ships to take the GI brides to the USA, on 26 January 1946. The youngest bride was 15 and the oldest 44. It was difficult for the GI brides to get to the USA after the war: the American government insisted that shipping the troops back took priority.

Source D

British girls dance with GIs at an American base.

Source E

Things to do

1 Why were American GIs stationed in Britain?

2 Look at Source A. What do you think the boys and the GI are saying to each other? Use the information in the caption as a starting point.

3 Sources C–E are all to do with British girls meeting American GIs.
For each source, work out what the girl's parents and British boyfriends might have felt.

4 Look at Source E and read the caption. What emotions do you think are going through the girls' minds? *Fear; excitement; sadness; hope?* Choose one or more of these emotions and explain your choice.

5 Did the stationing of GIs in Britain have a good or bad effect on the British people? Use all the sources and information in this unit to help you reach a decision.

By the end of April 1945 Germany was on the point of defeat. On 1 May Admiral Doenitz announced *our Führer, Adolf Hitler, has fallen. At the end of his struggle he met a hero's death.* In reality Hitler and his wife, Eva Braun, had both committed suicide in Hitler's bunker, deep under Berlin – though their bodies were never found. Hitler's death left Admiral Doenitz in charge and on 7 May he bowed to the inevitable and surrendered to the Allies. The war in the west was over. But what was to happen to Germany?

Another settlement

The harsh settlement imposed in the Treaty of Versailles at the end of the First World War was a major cause of the Second World War. The Germans felt that they had been unfairly blamed for causing the war. It was important to behave differently now the Second World War was over.

Germany was badly in need of help. Allied bombers had reduced many cities to little more than rubble and millions of people were desperate for proper food, clothing and shelter.

To add to the problems, hundreds of thousands of German refugees had fled from eastern Germany into Berlin. They knew the Soviet Red Army, advancing on Berlin from the east, was carrying out terrible acts of revenge for the atrocities committed by German troops in the Soviet Union. The refugees were fleeing west to avoid this.

On 25 April the Soviet forces met up with troops from Britain, France and the USA, in Berlin. Germany was occupied by the armies of the four major Allies. What would happen now?

The agreement

The Allied leaders had already given considerable thought to what should happen to Germany once the war was over. Roosevelt, Stalin and Churchill had met at Yalta in February 1945 and agreed that:

- Germany should be divided into four occupation zones, one controlled by Britain, one by the USA, one by France and one by the Soviet Union. The German capital, Berlin, would be divided in a similar way. This was to be a temporary solution until Germany recovered from the war.

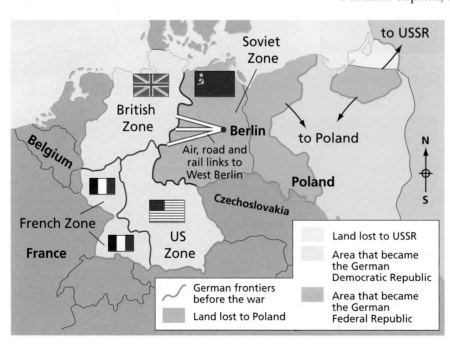

The division of Germany after the Second World War.

- The Allies would take goods and machinery from Germany as reparations for the cost of the war. So the Soviet Union began dismantling factories in its area of occupation and sending the equipment back to the Soviet Union.
- The countries that had been liberated from German occupation in eastern Europe would be allowed to have free elections to set up their own governments.

Not according to plan

Unfortunately things did not work out as planned. The Soviet Union was determined to see communist governments elected in eastern Europe, to provide 'friendly' nations between it and the West. This resulted in the setting up of what Churchill called the 'Iron Curtain' dividing communist eastern Europe from democratic western Europe. The zones of occupation stayed and in 1949 the British, French and American zones became the German Federal Republic (West Germany). The Soviet zone became the German Democratic Republic (East Germany). Berlin, which was in the Soviet zone, remained divided into four zones and in 1961 the Soviet Union built the Berlin Wall to stop Berliners crossing from one zone to another.

So the map of Europe had been redrawn between the communist East and democratic West. Each side now lined up on either side of the Iron Curtain to fight the 'Cold War' (see pages 68–9). It was only when that dispute ended in 1990 that the two Germanies were finally re-united.

Source A

Part of a speech made by ex-Prime Minister, Winston Churchill, in America in March 1946.

A shadow has fallen across the scenes so lately lighted by Allied victory. From Stettin in the Baltic to Trieste in the Adriatic an Iron Curtain has descended across the continent.

Source B

A German soldier sits amongst the rubble of Berlin at the end of the war.

Things to do

1 The war was over in May 1945. Why didn't the Allies just leave Germany alone at that point?

2 Why do you think that both Germany and the capital, Berlin, were split into four sections?

3 Why do you think the Soviet Union insisted on having communist governments elected in eastern Europe? (Hint: think about what had happened in Europe in the period 1917–45.)

4 a What did Churchill mean by the 'Iron Curtain'?

   b Why do you think he gave it that name?

Little Boy and Fat Man – unwelcome visitors

The Americans did not suffer heavy casualties invading Japan, because that invasion never took place. Instead President Truman decided to use a deadly new weapon which the Allies had been developing. For some years scientists in America had been working on the 'Manhattan Project'. They were trying to use recent scientific discoveries to produce an 'atomic bomb' which would be capable of destroying small cities. By late 1945 they were ready.

At 8.15 a.m. Colonel Paul Tibbets and his crew flew the B-29 bomber, the *Enola Gay*, above Hiroshima. They were carrying an atomic bomb, nick-named 'Little Boy'. As the bomb exploded, Tibbets cried 'My God, what have we done?' Below most of the city was destroyed and 80,000 people were killed. That number increased to 140,000 by the end of the year.

Terrifying though the consequences were, the Japanese government did not surrender. It was hoping to persuade the Soviet Union to negotiate peace terms with the Americans. So three days later the Americans dropped 'Fat Man' on Nagasaki and another 70,000 Japanese men, women and children were killed. The Japanese now surrendered, but had the USA been justified in what it had done?

Source B

Part of the order issued to drop the atomic bomb in August 1945.

TOP SECRET

To:
**General Carl Spaatz
Commanding General
United States Army Strategic Air Forces**

1 The 20th air force will deliver its first special bomb as soon as weather will permit visual bombing after about 3 August 1945. The target will be one of Hiroshima, Kokura, Niigata or Nagasaki. Additional aircraft will accompany the plane, carrying civilian scientific personnel to observe and record the effects of the bomb. The observing planes will stay several miles distant from the point of impact of the bomb.

2 Additional bombs will be delivered on the above targets as soon as they are made ready by project staff.

Damage caused by the bomb at Nagasaki

Area of damage:
6.7 square kilometres
Houses completely destroyed or burned: 12,900
Houses badly damaged: 5509
Number killed: 73,884
Number injured: 74,909

Source C

Henry Stimpson, who, as American Secretary of War, agreed to the dropping of the atomic bomb, explaining in 1947 why he believed it was the correct decision.

The Allies would have been faced with the enormous task of destroying an armed force of five million men and five thousand suicide aircraft. We estimated that if we were forced to invade, the major fighting would not end until the end of 1946 at the earliest and might be expected to cost over a million casualties to American forces alone.

Source D

A criticism made by the US Admiral Leahy in 1950. Leahy had been adviser to President Truman in 1945.

In my opinion the use of this barbarous weapon at Hiroshima and Nagasaki was of no material assistance in our war against Japan. The Japanese were already defeated and were ready to surrender because of the effective sea blockade and the successful bombing with conventional weapons.

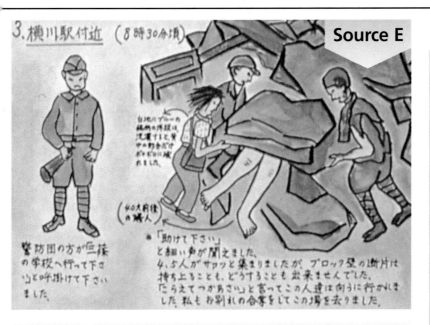

Source E

This picture was one of a number painted in 1975 by a survivor of the bomb, who is describing a scene she witnessed. The Japanese words tell of how a woman has asked for help, but people are unable to lift the concrete block off her. *Saying 'Forgive us' the others left her as she was. I prayed for her and then left also.*

Source F

A description of the fears of a young girl badly injured in the Hiroshima explosion.

Every so often someone searching amongst the wounded would pass by, and though it was agonising, she would raise her body slightly, whisper her name and address and beg them to contact her parents. Once she heard someone say, 'That poor girl is going to die' and from then on she determined to stay awake, afraid that if she let herself doze off, it would be her last sleep.

Source G

A Hiroshima father describing the death of his daughter.

My daughter had no burns and only minor external wounds, but on 4 September she suddenly became very sick. She had spots all over her body. Her hair began to fall out. She vomited small clumps of blood many times. After ten days of agony she died.

Source H

The scene at Hiroshima after the blast.

Things to do

1 What evidence can you find on pages 60 and 61 that:
   a the Americans knew how much damage the bombs would cause
   b there might be effects which the Americans had not considered?

2 What arguments can you find to suggest that the Americans:
   a were justified in what they did
   b were not justified in what they did?

3 'I don't know what all the fuss is about. Everyone knew that they had no choice.'
   Do you agree with this comment on the dropping of the bomb by the USA?

4 If you were President Truman, would you have dropped the bomb? Give reasons to explain your decision.

What was the Holocaust?

The Holocaust was the Nazi answer to the fact that the ever-expanding Nazi state was full of 'undesirable' people. These people had to be destroyed. 'Holocaust' means 'wholesale destruction'.

Who were the undesirables?

Most undesirable were people who were not 'Aryan' – Aryans had 'purely' German blood. The most undesirable people of all to Nazis were the Jews. Even before the Nazis got into power, they made their anti-Jewish feelings clear. Once in power they began to make life hard for Jews, encouraging them to leave Germany. Laws, like the 1935 Nuremberg Laws, stopped Jews from working in professions such as teaching and law. They also made rules against Jews owning dogs and using public parks or swimming pools.

While Jews were the main targets, there were other undesirables too. Black people, the physically and mentally handicapped, homosexuals, gypsies and otherwise acceptable Germans who spoke out against the Nazis were all undesirable too.

What happened to them?

Many mentally and physically handicapped people were shut up in asylums, where some of them were experimented on and killed. Many black people were sterilised (operated on so they could not have children). Gypsies, homosexuals, black people, non-Aryans and political opponents were shut up in concentration camps. Jews who remained in Germany were put into concentration camps or herded into city ghettos – walled-off areas of the city for Jews only (set up mostly in Polish towns). Jews from all walks of life were crammed into these ghettos.

What was a concentration camp?

Concentration camps were places where 'undesirable' people were herded together. Other countries, like America and Britain, had used camps like this for captured enemy soldiers in wartime. Nazi concentration camps were to have a very different purpose, as we will see.

Removing those who starved to death in the Warsaw Ghetto. The ghetto is behind the wall.

Source A

Perec Zylberberg worked as a weaver. This photo, taken in the ghetto at the time, shows him learning how to weave.

Esther and Perec Zylberberg

The numbers involved in the Holocaust are huge. It is easy to lose sight of real people. So we will follow two people through it – Esther and Perec Zylberberg. They lived in Lodz, Poland. The Nazis set up the first ghetto in Lodz in May 1940. Perec was 16; Esther was 12.

Lodz Ghetto

The ghetto was in the most run-down part of the city. It was mostly one-room flats. There were 31,720 of these flats. Only 700 had running water. About 200,000 Jews were crammed into the ghetto. The Nazis sent thousands more Jews there, from all over the lands occupied by the Nazis. They began to move people out, too. No one knew where these people were going. They were told they were being resettled, on farmland, outside the Nazi state. They had to pay for tickets and were told to take their valuables with them.

Source B

Perec Zylberberg worked as a weaver. This photo, taken in the ghetto at the time, shows him learning how to weave.

ESTHER AND PEREC ZYLBERBERG

The Germans attacked Poland on 1 September, 1939. They bombed several places at once, including Lodz. The army reached the city on 8 September.

Perec: *We went to visit relatives who lived near the city centre. As we came to the city centre the first motorbike came into view. The thing that struck me was the clapping when they arrived. It was all those Germans who had been living in Poland, as Poles. So they had a ready-made occupation machine. My mother said Germans were hard, but fair. A lot of people of her generation thought like that.*

Esther: *We were terrorised from the very beginning, before the ghetto was set up. I was very scared, but I also had a kind of childish excitement that 'It's going to be over soon and my, won't there be a lot to talk about!' The French and British were in the war now. The French had the best army and the British ruled the seas. The first painful thing for us as a family was that my father had to flee, because he was an active member of the **Bund**. My brother David went too, to the Russian army. I never saw them again.*

The Chronicle

The people of Lodz kept day-by-day secret records which survived the war. They tell us about conditions in the ghetto at the time. They also tell us of the hopes people had that the Nazis would soon be beaten, or that they would accept the Jews as useful and treat them better so they could work harder. They did not know what was about to happen.

Things to do

1 a What does Holocaust mean?
  b Which people were 'undesirable'?

2 a What is a ghetto?
  b Why do you think the Nazis set up Jewish ghettos?

3 What do Esther and Perec say that suggests that Jews at the time thought they would be able to get by under German rule?

The Final Solution

Many Jews died in the ghettos, of sickness or starvation, but they were not dying quickly enough for many Nazis. As the army advanced on Russia, special killing squads were sent to kill Jews in newly-captured areas. But this was 'a waste of bullets' and still too slow. So in 1941 the Nazis used camps to kill Jews – their Final Solution to the problem. Camps were set up in isolated places which could be reached by railway. There were three sorts:

- **concentration camps:** prison camps. Here, prisoners mostly died from sickness, starvation and overwork.
- **labour camps:** larger camps where prisoners were used as slave labour in factories built nearby. Conditions were harsher, but, again, people mainly died from starvation, sickness and overwork.
- **death camps:** camps for killing people as quickly and economically as possible.

Camps were sometimes combined for efficiency. So Auschwitz had a concentration camp (Auschwitz I), a death camp (Auschwitz II/Birkenau) and a labour camp with factories (Auschwitz III).

Source C

From the *Chronicle* of the Lodz ghetto. Jews taken from the ghetto were told they would be 'resettled' outside the Nazi state. But they suspected something more sinister was going on.

Saturday, 15 July 1944: Today the Council Elder was told to halt resettlement. People hugged in the streets; kissed in the workshops. 'Resettlement's over!' No one thought whether this was only a brief interruption or a final halt to the transports. One thing is certain: no transport is being prepared for Monday. The ghetto has lost the habit of thinking more than a few hours ahead.

The industry of death

One of the most gruesome things about the death camps is how the Nazis kept 'improving' them. The first people taken from the Lodz ghetto (from January 1942 onwards) were taken to Chelmno death camp. In four months 54,979 Jews left Lodz to die at Chelmno. They were loaded into sealed vans and gassed with exhaust fumes. But this was still not efficient enough. And it used up petrol. In July 1944 the transports from Lodz stopped. Chelmno had been shut down. A new and more efficient system had been set up: gas chambers. The next transports from Lodz went to Auschwitz and its death camp, Birkenau. The Nazis now re-used every part of the people they murdered – their clothing, their hair, their teeth, their ashes. They tried to re-use their fat, too. But people who are starving to death have none.

The Nazi camps.

Source D

The platform at Auschwitz where people were divided up into groups. Some went to the labour camp. Others went straight to the death camp, Auschwitz/Birkenau. This is what happened to Esther's mother, Sara Zylberberg.

Esther: *The most painful moments in the ghetto were the mass deportations. Most of my friends were disappearing. All the people who were deported were never heard of again. Clothing started to arrive back, marked with names. People found their relatives' clothes.* Esther and her mother were deported together, to Auschwitz. *We had been under Nazi occupation for so long, and suffered degradation, hunger and disease, but we were not prepared for what Auschwitz was. We thought we were being sent to another place of work. When we arrived we said 'where are we?' The railway people said 'You mean you don't know what this place is?' I had seen the barbed wire, people looking mad. We did not think we would stop there. It looked like a lunatic asylum. They gave us a tin of food on arrival, to eat while we were being pushed towards selection. This was the most painful moment, which I have never got over – separation from my mother.*

Perec: *The deportations got more frequent. There were already fears about what they meant. Work was a passport to staying on. I managed to get my mother and my sister into the carpet-making plant. We were undernourished, disease-ridden, in constant fear of almost everything.* Perec was 19 when he was transported to a labour camp at Czestochowa. *The work was hard. There weren't many machines, we did most of the hauling of machine parts. The German guards carried whips and there were regular whippings, but we were not beaten too often. It was a business-like slave compound. There were Germans in charge, but they set up Jewish foremen and police. On 15 January 1945 we were woken early, given some bread and coffee and told to pack our belongings.* The Russians were close to Czestochowa. The workers marched deeper into Germany, to Buchenwald labour camp. It had all sorts of 'undesirables', even US war prisoners. *We were almost shoeless and dressed in tattered trousers, with no underwear or coats. The frosts were terrible. We had to clear the rubble when a nearby city was bombed. It was the first time I had seen ordinary Germans. Now and again a woman would give us a potato or a piece of bread.*

Things to do

'The Jews in the camps did fight back. But they were held back by a variety of factors: physical weakness, sickness, lack of weapons, the isolation of camps, disbelief and hope.' List each of these things. Say how they might have stopped people from fighting back. Use evidence from these pages in your answer.

Liberation and after

As the Russians advanced on Germany, camps in Poland (including Auschwitz) were closed down. People were marched to camps closer to the centre of Germany. Many died on the way. Allied soldiers who reached the camps found only those few who had hidden or had been left to die. They found piles of dead bodies, huge mounds marking mass graves and vast heaps of ashes with fragments of bones. They began to realise the scale of the killing.

What happened to the survivors?

The Nazis nearly wiped out all Jews in Nazi-occupied areas. But there were survivors. They were cared for in hospitals until they could be moved. Then they had to cope with the rest of their lives. Most had lost many relatives. They had lost their homes, their possessions, their health. Many of the children were taken to other countries and found homes and work. But they had a great deal to adjust to. Most people were kind, but could not understand what the children had lived through. The emphasis was on getting them working, not replacing the years of schooling they had lost.

Source F

The British journalist Patrick Gordon Walker wrote this account of Belsen, a labour camp, not a death camp. (Esther Zylberberg was marched here from Auschwitz.)

Corpses in every state of decay were lying around, piled on top of each other in heaps. People, walking skeletons, were falling dead all around. One woman came up to a soldier and asked for milk for her baby. The man took the baby and saw it had been dead for days, black in the face and shrivelled up. She went on begging for milk. So he poured some on the dead lips. The mother carried the baby off, stumbled and fell dead after a few yards.

Five thousand people have died here in nine days. We found an Englishman, half dead. He had a bullet in his back. He had been shot by a guard while crawling about days before. Everywhere there was the smell of death. Many people have typhus and dysentery. Most of the girls here are Jews from Auschwitz. Over and over I hear the same story of the parades where people were picked out for the gas chambers. To you at home, this is one camp. There are many more. This is what you are fighting. None of this is propaganda. It is the simple truth.

Source E

Just one of the hundreds of mass graves found by Allies in Nazi concentration camps.

Source G

Some of Esther's and Perec's family, before Esther was born. Perec (the baby on the right) is the only one from this photo who survived the Holocaust.

Esther and Perec made it through the Holocaust. They nearly didn't. Both were moved on ahead of the advancing Allied armies. Both were ill when their camps were liberated. The sick were dumped in 'hospitals' to die.

Perec was moved by train.

Perec: *We passed through bombed-out cities. At Chemnitz we could see from the open trucks right across the bombed buildings to the other side of the city. It warmed our hearts. There is a sort of fog surrounding that journey in my memory. I seem to remember eating grass, leaves, bark. The trains went backwards and forwards and we lost count of the days and nights. Eventually we must have got somewhere. I remember people yelling, commands. We disembarked. I heard about half the transport died, that some dead were eaten. I don't remember seeing that, but that's what I heard. Then I wasn't in a freight car. I was in a building with bunks. I don't know who was in charge, Red Cross or Germans. There were quite a few nurses, I remember that. I remember being in a bed, clinging to a piece of bread. I kept grabbing for it and people calmed me down, showed it to me. A nurse told me that I had typhus and was in a clinic. The next thing I remember is a tank outside the window and thinking: the Allies are here.*

Perec was one of 732 young people taken to England. They went to hostels in the Lake District and then to homes all over the country. Perec tried to track down his family. Only Esther could be found. Perec moved to Canada in 1958 and set up in the clothing business. He still lives there.

Esther: *When I came to, everyone was going mad. There was murder in everyone's hearts, probably in mine too. Despite the fact that I knew what had happened to my mother, I had to keep on believing that somehow it wasn't true. I prayed with all my might, I don't know who to, probably myself, 'please let me not be damaged for the whole of my life. Let me keep some love for people.'*

Esther was taken to Sweden. In April 1947 she came to England.

I lived with an elderly Jewish couple. They treated me well, but could not really understand me. I longed to continue my education, to train as a nurse, but no one was prepared to give me my keep while I tried to replace my lost years.

Esther married another Holocaust survivor, Stasiek Brunstein. They had two children. Esther now lives in London.

Things to do

Perec Zylberberg says of the adults who looked after the children who arrived in England: *Very little was ever said about the atrocities of the war, about our personal experiences.* Why do you think people did not talk to the children about what they had gone through?

Britain and the USA had always been uneasy in an alliance with the USSR because of their political differences. Less than a year after winning the Second World War, they were openly talking about the USSR as an enemy. For over 40 years the two sides were so hostile to each other that historians call it 'the Cold War' – 'Cold' because they never actually went to war.

Why were they hostile?

The main reason for hostility was their different economic and political systems. The USSR was a communist state. The USA and Britain were capitalist states. Many people, in both countries, believed communism and capitalism could not exist alongside each other for long. One system would take over the other. Both sides were determined not to be taken over.

Buffer zones

In the USSR, Stalin wanted a **buffer zone** – friendly countries between the USSR and possible enemies in the west. The USSR had been invaded from the west before. British, French and US troops had invaded to help the anti-communists in the Civil War, in 1919 and 1920. Hitler had invaded the USSR in 1941. Stalin set up 'satellite states' between the USSR and the West. They governed themselves, but were communist and dominated by the USSR. Anyone invading the USSR from the west would have to invade these countries first.

One goes, they all go

The USA and Britain feared communism would spread to the West through eastern Europe. Some leaders believed the 'domino theory'. They felt if one country became communist, it would set off another and another. It would be like knocking over the first in a line of dominoes – each domino would knock the next one over. They were desperate to stop any country becoming the first communist domino.

Eastern European communist governments set up: Yugoslavia (1945), Bulgaria (1947), Poland, Czechoslovakia, Hungary, Romania (1948).

Vietnam, 1959–75: The USA sent money, weapons and troops to South Vietnam to help the government fight communist **guerrillas** who were backed by the North Vietnamese. The US troops could not defeat the communist guerrillas, so withdrew in 1973. Two years later South Vietnam became a communist state.

Cuba, 1962: Cuba became a communist country in 1959, after a revolution led by Fidel Castro. The Soviets asked Castro to let them build a missile base in Cuba. This would put most of the USA in range of Soviet missiles. The USA ordered a naval blockade of Cuba to stop the missiles arriving. For a while it looked as if nuclear war would break out. At the last minute the USSR climbed down and abandoned the plans for a missile base.

Czechoslovakia, 1968; Poland, 1981: There was opposition to communist rule in both countries. The opposition was crushed each time with the help of Soviet troops.

The collapse of eastern European communism, 1989: Reforms in the USSR lessened communist power. Revolutions in satellite countries kicked out communist governments. First went Poland, then East Germany, Hungary, Czechoslovakia, Bulgaria and Romania. In December the Soviet leader, Gorbachev, and the US President, Bush, declared the Cold War over. Later that month the demolition of the Berlin Wall began.

NATO, 1949: The North Atlantic Treaty Organisation was an alliance between the USA, Britain, France, Canada, Portugal, Norway, Belgium, the Netherlands and Italy. They promised to defend each other against attack from the USSR.

People's Republic of China, 1949: The Chinese Communist Party (with help from the USSR) won the Chinese Civil War. China became a communist country, but did not have good relations with the USSR.

The division of Germany, 1949: At the end of the Second World War, the USSR occupied one half of Germany. Britain, France and the USA occupied the other. Eventually Germany became two countries: communist East Germany and capitalist West Germany.

The Korean War, 1950–3: After the Second World War the USA occupied South Korea; the USSR, North Korea. Each set up its own government. The communist North Koreans invaded the south. The USA and its allies sent troops to help South Korea. China sent troops to the north. The two sides made peace in 1953, agreeing to make two separate countries.

The Warsaw Pact, 1955: After West Germany was allowed to join NATO in 1955, the USSR and its allies (Romania, Poland, East Germany, Bulgaria, Czechoslovakia and Hungary) set up the Warsaw Pact – an alliance against the Western powers.

N.A.T.O. countries

Warsaw Pact countries

U.S.A

CANADA

North Pole +

New York

CHINA

U S S R

I N D I A

PAKISTAN

EASTERN EUROPE

Paris Vienna

Geneva

The Berlin Wall, 1961: So many people were escaping from East to West Germany in Berlin (which was itself divided between East and West Germany) that the East German government built a wall with guardposts to stop it. To most people this was the most obvious symbol of the Cold War.

The Hungarian Rising, 1956: Not all satellite states were happy. Many people in Hungary wanted more freedom than their communist government gave them. They rebelled. After five days of fighting, Soviet troops moved into Hungary and crushed the rising. Hungary stayed communist and in the Warsaw Pact.

Things to do

1 Draw a timeline from 1945 to 1990. Mark the events of the Cold War on it.

2 Draw up a table like the one shown here. For each event on this page, say if you think it had anything to do with domino theory or the idea of a buffer zone, or both. The first one has been done for you.

Event	Buffer zone	Domino theory
Division of Germany	Yes: USSR wanted East Germany as a buffer zone	Yes: USA and Britain wanted to stop West Germany from becoming communist

The box on Cuba, 1962, on page 68, says: *The USA ordered a naval blockade of Cuba.* It sounds like a simple decision, easily made. But it was only made after days of almost constant discussion, consultation with US allies and negotiations with the USSR. Tapes of the discussions, made by President Kennedy, were made public in 1997. They give us an insight into the uncertainty and disagreement behind the final statement of government policy. During the crisis, no one knew what would happen. Both sides had to consider the possibility of nuclear war. Both sides wanted to avoid this. But they also wanted to avoid giving in.

What sparked off the crisis?

On 16 October 1962, US planes took secret photos that showed Russian missiles, capable of carrying nuclear warheads, on the island of Cuba. For the first time in history the USA would be within reach of Russian nuclear missiles. Frantic debate followed between the US President and his advisers about what to do.

What happened?

After days of discussion, consultation with experts and US allies and negotiations with the USSR, the President and his advisers reached a decision. On 22 October they ordered a naval blockade of Cuba. After several tense days, where there was a serious possibilty of nuclear war, the USSR backed down. The next page gives part of the debate on the first day of the crisis.

The crisis had so concerned the leaders of the USSR and the USA that in 1963 they agreed to set up a direct telephone link between Moscow and Washington, now called the 'hot-line'.

Things to do

1 a What options were President Kennedy and his advisers considering?
 b What did they actually do on 22 October?
 c Was this one of the three options discussed on day one?
 d So why do you think this happened?

2 a List the people who spoke in the extract on page 71, saying what they wanted to do and why.
 b Pick one person and say what you think their response to the suggestion of just a blockade would be, and why you think this.

3 Does Source A show the Americans were right to fear a nuclear attack?

Source A

CHERRY PICKER

LAUNCH PAD WITH ERECTOR

LAUNCH PAD WITH ERECTOR

MISSILE READY BLDGS.

OXIDIZER VEHICLES

FUELING VEHICLES

One of the pictures that started it all. Many of them are hard to interpret, but in this one you can see the missile carriers clearly. The labels were put on at the time by the Americans.

MRBM = Medium Range Ballistic Missile.

16 OCTOBER MORNING

Lundahl: *There's a missile launch site and 2 new military encampments on the southern edge of Sierra del Rosario.*

President Kennedy: *How do you know it's a missile?*

Lundahl: *The length, sir.*

President Kennedy: *Is it ready to be fired?*

Graybeal: *No sir.*

President Kennedy: *How long have we got?*

Graybeal: *If the equipment's checked sir, you're talking about a matter of hours.*

Rusk: *Do we assume these are nuclear?*

McNamarra: *There's no question about that. We don't know where the warheads are, how soon they can be armed. It could take hours, even days, to be ready.*

Rusk: *Sir, this is serious. We have to get rid of this base. Do we do an unannounced strike, or build up pressure until the other side has to act or give in? We could make a quick strike – not invade, or start a war, make it clear we were just wiping out the base. Or we can eliminate the problem by eliminating the whole island. Or we could take the political route. Make it clear we know what's going on. Demand to inspect the site. Whatever we do, we should call up troops. We need to get onto NATO. Blockade Cuba. No flights; get the British to stop trade. We face a situation that could well lead to general war.*

McNamarra: *If we're going to bomb these installations, it has to be before they are armed. There's no knowing when that will be. We'll have to hit the missile sites, air bases, any hidden aircraft and possible nuclear storage sites. This would be a big strike. We'd kill a lot of Cubans, 2–3000. We would have to follow up, invade.*

President Kennedy: *So you're talking about:*

1 *Strike just the bases.*
2 *Strike bases, airfields and anything else connected with the missile sites.*
3 *Do that and blockade as well.*

There's the question of allied consultation. Don't

Who's who?

This list covers those people speaking in this extract. Others were involved in the debates.

Political advisors: Robert Kennedy (the President's brother), Robert McNamarra (Secretary of Defense), Dean Rusk (Secretary of State).

Military advisors: General Maxwell Taylor, Arthur Lundahl (an expert on interpreting photographs), Sidney Graybeal (a missile expert).

think it'll be a lot of use. Probably ought to tell them, though, night before.

Robert Kennedy: *We have to decide whether to invade. If we do the full air strike, we'll kill a lot of people. So the Russians will either send in more missiles or strike our missiles in Turkey or Iran.*

Rusk: *You might as well. Do the whole job.*

President Kennedy: *We need to work out what we need to do in the next 24 hrs to be ready for any option. Let's meet tonight, after you've consulted. As we don't know how soon the missiles can be ready, we have to start preparing to take them out. Because that's what we're going to do anyway. We're certainly going to do No 1. We're going to take out these missiles.*

16 OCTOBER EVENING

McNamarra: *We could start with a limited air attack. But the Soviets would respond, militarily, somewhere in the world. It may be worth that price. But we must recognize that the price is there. And we should be ready to mobilize our troops to counter it.*

President Kennedy: *The chances of it becoming a broader struggle increase each time you step it up. If you do all those air strikes, then you might as well invade.*

Taylor: *I don't think we should invade.*

McNamarra: *Circumstances might force us to. And we might be forced to blockade.*

Robert Kennedy: *Then you'd have to sink Russian ships and submarines. Shouldn't we get it over with and take our losses? Hell, if he sticks those kinds of missiles in after the warning then he's gonna get a war, when he does. So...*

McNamarra: *Which supports the point I was making. We ought to get the options down and work out the consequences.*

3.3 EUROPEANS GO HOME

Have you ever wondered why so many people in the world speak English, French or Spanish? The answer lies in the fact that until recently each of the major European countries had an overseas empire. Most of the Spanish Empire had gained independence by 1900, but when the Second World War broke out in 1939, Britain and France still had vast empires, covering over a quarter of the world. Within the next 30 years those empires vanished. Why?

The effects of the Second World War (1939–45)

In 1940 German troops occupied much of western Europe and threatened to invade Britain. People living in the colonies of the defeated nations watched these developments with interest. They had always thought their European masters were mighty nations that could not be challenged. Now they saw that this was not the case. This led many of them to lose respect for Europeans and consider how best to win back their independence.

For some countries the answer was already at hand. The Japanese realised that the European countries were fighting for their own survival and could not protect their colonies. So in South-East Asia, Japan invaded and occupied European colonies. At first the Japanese were welcomed as liberators, but their brutal treatment of the local inhabitants soon changed this. When Japan was defeated and the Europeans returned, they found that their colonies were no longer prepared to be ruled by foreigners. Independence was soon to follow, though sometimes only after fierce fighting.

Source A

Mahatma Gandhi. He was so respected in India that even when he was imprisoned by the British in 1928 for encouraging opposition to their rule, the judge described him as *in a different category from any person I have ever tried, or am likely to try.*

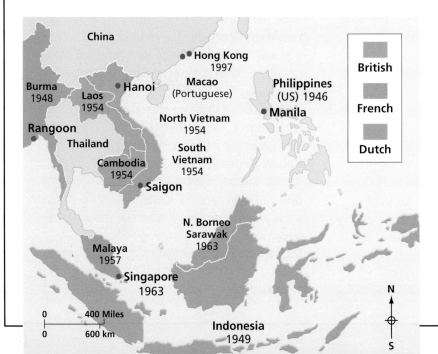

How South-East Asia became independent.

Economic problems

Britain and France won the war, but at a great economic cost. In 1945 Britain was in debt to the USA and found it hard to pay to run an empire. The new Labour government, elected in 1945, wanted to make India independent, but was worried about violence between Muslims and Hindus. In the end the subcontinent was divided into India (mainly Hindu) and Pakistan (mainly Muslim). Ceylon (now Sri Lanka) also became independent.

The growth of nationalism

One of the benefits of European rule was that it brought widespread education to local people. But education introduced the idea that people should govern themselves. This led **nationalist** leaders (such as Gandhi in India, and Jomo Kenyatta in Kenya) to ask why this did not apply to their own countries. They carried out campaigns for independence and used mistakes made by Europeans, such as the Amritsar Massacre (see pages 74–5), to win support for their cause.

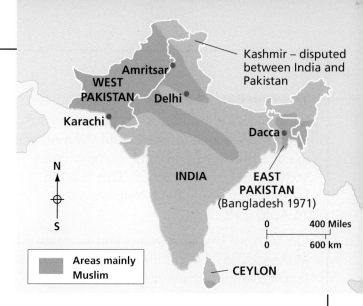

India after independence.

In Africa, in particular, freedom fighters began to carry out wars against their European masters, and independence, in places such as Algeria and Indonesia, was won only after fierce fighting.

By 1970 the European empires were gone. Some small remnants of empire remained – mostly places such as St Helena and Montserrat, financed by European countries – and not wanting independence.

How Africa became independent.

Things to do

1 What do you think might be the advantages of an empire for:
   a the ruling country
   b the people of the colony?

2 What do you think the judge meant in Source A? Try to find out why Gandhi was so well respected.

3 Why did European empires come to an end in the twentieth century?

4 Do you think that one country owning and ruling another country can ever be justified?

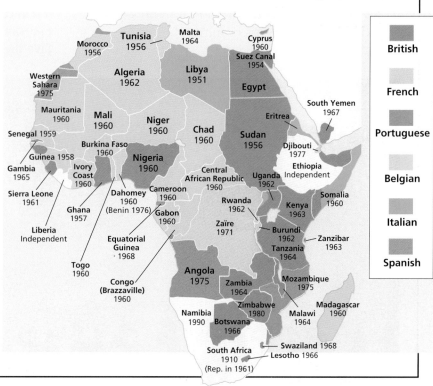

The Amritsar Massacre

By 1919 many Indians were determined to win independence from Britain. Demonstrations against British rule became common and sometimes led to violence. This is what happened in the city of Amritsar on 13 April 1919.

On 10 April five Europeans had been murdered in the city. As a result the British General Dyer banned all public meetings in the area.

Despite this a crowd of over 5000 Indians met in an area known as the Jallianwala Bagh to hear speeches criticising the British. Although the meeting was peaceful and contained large numbers of men, women and children, General Dyer was determined to break it up. He took his troops to the Jallianwala Bagh and positioned them on high ground near the narrow entrance. He ordered his troops to open fire on the crowd without warning.

The Jallianwala Bagh was surrounded by a wall five feet high and there were few exits. Official British figures state that nearly two thousand men, women and children were wounded or killed. The British set up the Hunter Committee to investigate the incident and General Dyer was dismissed from his command.

Source C

An extract from *The Times*, 27 May 1920.

General Dyer, with a very small force, opened fire upon a dense crowd assembled in a confined space. His soldiers fired 1650 times, killing 379 persons and possibly wounding three times as many. The government has since stated that although there were problems in the area, Dyer was not entitled to select for punishment an unarmed crowd which had committed no acts of violence, had made no attempts to oppose him by force, and many of whom must have been unaware that they were breaking his order.

Source D

An extract from the *Daily Mail*, 4 May 1920.

**TINY LOYAL FORCE AGAINST
GREAT CROWD OF INDIANS**

General Dyer issued orders against violence and damage to property, and against meetings of more than four people. Despite this, the Indians gathered in large numbers at Jallianwala Bagh – estimates vary between 5000 and 30,000. It was then that Dyer, who was in command of a little force of less than a hundred soldiers and two armoured cars, gave the order to fire.

Source B

A scene from the film *Gandhi* showing Dyer's troops firing on the crowd.

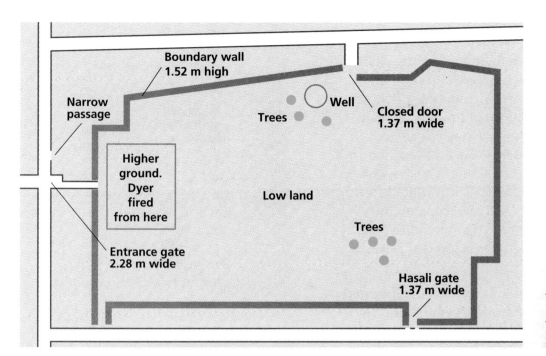

The Jallianwala Bagh.

Labels in diagram:
Boundary wall 1.52 m high
Narrow passage
Trees
Well
Closed door 1.37 m wide
Higher ground. Dyer fired from here
Low land
Entrance gate 2.28 m wide
Trees
Hasali gate 1.37 m wide

Source E

Part of an interview with General Dyer in the *Daily Mail* on 4 May 1920.

I had to shoot. I had thirty seconds to make up my mind about what action to take. What would have happened if I had not shot? I and my little force would have been swept away and then what would have happened?

Source F

Part of the evidence given by General Dyer to the Hunter Committee.

Question: You did not issue a warning to the crowd to disperse before you opened fire. Did you think you were going to be attacked?

Dyer: The situation in the area was very serious. It was no longer a question of merely dispersing the crowd. I had to produce a sufficient impression of strength not only on those who were there, but throughout that part of India.

Question: When did you decide to fire?

Dyer: When I first heard of the meeting.

Question: If the entrance into the Jallianwala Bagh had been wide enough to allow your armoured cars in, would you have used their machine guns on the crowd?

Dyer: I think, probably, yes.

Things to do

1 a Make a list of all the different reasons you can find on these pages for General Dyer opening fire on the crowd in the Jallianwala Bagh.
  b For each reason:
  • write beside it by whom it was given
  • say whether you have any particular reason to doubt or believe it.

2 The accounts on these pages have different numbers for those killed and wounded. Why do you think this is?

3 From what you have read on these pages, do you think General Dyer should have been dismissed? Explain your answer.

3.4 THE WAR IN VIETNAM

Why was there a war?

In 1954 North Vietnam and South Vietnam gained their independence from France. North Vietnam was a communist country led by Ho Chi Minh, but South Vietnam was anti-communist. However, inside South Vietnam there was a group of armed rebels called the Vietcong. These were communist supporters who wanted to overthrow their own government and make South Vietnam a communist country. Not surprisingly they received support from North Vietnam.

Many people in South Vietnam supported the Vietcong. Their government, led by President Ngo Dingh Diem, was corrupt and had little interest in improving the lives of its people. But the Americans were keen supporters of Diem. He was strongly anti-communist, and so in their eyes was an ideal person to govern South Vietnam.

The domino theory

One of the reasons why the United States was so keen to prevent South Vietnam becoming a communist country was that it feared that once South Vietnam fell to communism, other countries would soon follow. This is called the domino theory, because it is like a collection of upright dominoes falling one after the other.

South East Asia during the Vietnam War.

As you read on pages 68–9 the Americans had been trying to prevent the spread of communism in Europe. Now it looked as if Asia, too, was under threat and the Americans were determined to defend it against communism.

In 1955 the United States began sending 'military advisers', weapons and supplies into Vietnam to help President Diem. Despite the assassination of Diem in 1963, the new American President, Lyndon Johnson, decided to step up American help for the new South Vietnamese government.

The domino theory.

The war hots up

By the late 1960s the Americans had over half a million troops in Vietnam fighting the Vietcong and North Vietnam, which was giving the Vietcong supplies. The Americans had the latest equipment such as rocket launchers and helicopter gunships, but the Vietcong did not fight open battles, where these weapons could be used. Instead they fought a guerrilla war – carrying out acts of sabotage on American bases, ambushing soldiers on patrol and setting up booby traps. Then they melted back into the jungle where the Americans could not find them.

These methods made the American soldiers very frustrated, as they were usually unable to identify who had carried out the attacks. Sometimes they took their revenge on suspected Vietcong hideouts but ended up killing innocent men, women and children.

To stop North Vietnam supplying the Vietcong down a jungle pathway called the Ho Chi Minh Trail, the Americans carried out a huge bombing campaign on North Vietnam's capital, Hanoi. American planes also dropped napalm to burn back the jungle and chemicals to take the leaves off the trees. These chemicals also killed animals and people. Whole villages were moved behind barbed wire to prevent contact with the Vietcong, but support for the communists did not decline.

Time to get out

By 1968 the United States was spending $30,000 million dollars a year and 300 of its soldiers were dying each week. At home there were huge demonstrations against the war, fuelled by news of atrocities carried out by American soldiers and pictures on television of the Vietcong attacking the American Embassy in the South Vietnamese capital, Saigon. President Nixon decided to withdraw American troops. In 1973 he managed to arrange a cease-fire between North and South Vietnam and brought the American soldiers home. Two years later North Vietnam invaded South Vietnam and united the two countries under the communist flag.

Source A

American soldiers on patrol encounter bamboo spikes laid by the Vietcong, as described in Source B.

Source B

A member of the Vietcong describes the best way to fight the Americans.

Let me tell you how we fought the Americans. We knew that we did not have the weapons to fight them in the open, so we had to fight another way. For instance, we would put many pieces of sharp bamboo in the ground near the paths the Americans walked on. Then we would shoot at the Americans when they were on the paths. They jumped off the paths and onto the bamboo and got very hurt.

Then the Americans always did the same thing. They would be very angry and might kill some people, or shoot up some houses or have a big military operation in the area. They never found us, but made many enemies when they did these things. That was the way to fight the Americans.

The My Lai Massacre

On 16 March 1968 a group of 150 soldiers and 5 officers from the American army were landed by helicopter near the South Vietnamese village of My Lai. The soldiers had been given instructions to ensure that the village contained no members of the Vietcong. The soldiers were surprised to find that their landing did not attract Vietcong fire and that there appeared to be no sign of Vietcong in the area.

The senior officer, Lieutenant William Calley, led his troops into the village and ordered that all the inhabitants were to be rounded up. As the soldiers searched the village, some of the women were raped and other civilians were gunned down. A group of old men, women and children were herded together and shot dead.

By the time the Americans left the village, an estimated 150 unarmed civilians had been killed.

What they said about the Massacre

Source C

An account of the attack from a villager who survived.

Nothing was happening here. It was a very quiet life. Then the helicopters came and all the troops surrounded us. They were firing their guns and the people were dying. Oh it was horrible! I pushed my son into the paddy field and lay on top of him. Corpses fell on top of us. I told him. 'Don't cry and see if we can survive.' I lifted my head and saw Americans pointing in all directions. The people who were still alive were shot again and again. I hate the Americans. I shall never forgive them.

A photograph shows some of the dead at My Lai.

Source D

Source E

An army sergeant comments on the purpose of the attack.

The understanding, or the order that was given, was to kill everyone in that village. Someone asked if that meant everyone. Those people, the women, the kids, the old men, were Vietcong or they were sympathetic to the Vietcong. It was quite clear that no one was to be spared in that village.

Source H

An American soldier comments on the problems faced by the US army in Vietnam.

You know you had little kids in Vietnam who would shoot you in the back as you walked away. I couldn't work out which people were the enemy. All of them looked the same, North Vietnamese and South Vietnamese. How could I tell?

Source F

Comments made by Lieutenant William Calley at his trial. Calley was the only person to be convicted for the massacre at My Lai. He was given a life sentence for murder, but released after three days on the instructions of President Nixon.

My troops were being massacred in Vietnam by an enemy they could not see. The enemy was communism. When I came face to face with it, I had to put the lives of my own troops first.

Source G

Survivors of My Lai being comforted after the massacre.

Things to do

1 Who was fighting whom in Vietnam?

2 Why did the Americans become involved in fighting in Vietnam?

3 Although they had better weapons, why did they find it so difficult to defeat the Vietcong?

4 Look back at page 77. Explain why the tactics used by the Vietcong in Source B would have been so effective.

5 Why did American troops launch a raid on My Lai?

6 Killing women and children was obviously wrong. How could the American army justify what happened?

7 If the attack on My Lai was so bad, how can you explain the fact that:

a William Calley was the only man convicted of a crime at My Lai

b he was released from prison after only three days?

3.5 THE UNITED NATIONS: AN ORGANISATION FOR PEACE?

The Second World War horrified people by its terrible loss of life and destruction. The League of Nations, an organisation set up at the end of the First World War, had failed to stop a second slide into devastating conflict. In 1945, shortly after the end of the Second World War, representatives from 50 countries met in San Francisco. They were setting up an organisation which, they were determined, would this time keep world peace and enable people to live their lives to the full.

Source A

This is the way in which the United Nations was organised.

United Nations Secretary General

Runs the UN aided by officials from all the member states.

Security Council

- Takes day-to-day action on behalf of the General Assembly.
- 15 members – the five great powers (UK, USA, CIS, France, China) and ten other nations elected for two years at a time.
- All decisions have to be carried by nine members voting YES and none of the Great Powers voting NO (the veto).

General Assembly

The parliament of the United Nations.
- Each member state has one vote.
- Meets once a year in September.
- Special meetings can be held in an emergency.
- Important matters decided by a two-thirds majority; other decisions by a simple majority.

UN ORGANIZATIONS AND AGENCIES

Other organizations and agencies do much of the most valuable work of the UN, such as WHO (health) and UNESCO (education).

Source B

The United Nations' Charter.

WE, THE PEOPLES OF THE UNITED NATIONS, ARE DETERMINED
- to save succeeding generations from the scourge of war which twice in our lifetime has brought untold sorrow to mankind,
- to reaffirm faith in fundamental human rights, in the dignity and worth of the human person, in the equal rights of men and women and of nations large and small,
- to establish respect for treaties and international law,
- to promote social progress and better standards of life in larger freedom,

AND FOR THESE ENDS
- to practise tolerance and live together in peace with one another,
- to unite our strength to maintain international peace and security,
- to ensure that armed force shall not be used save in the common interest,
- to help the economic and social advancement of all peoples.

A cartoon published in 1945.

Source C is

RULE: All ... to play together, but not so as to cramp any player's style. (That would be unrealistic)

"A FINE TEAM – BUT COULD DO WITH A DASH OF UNITY....."

The WHO campaign to rid the world of smallpox, 1967.

The United Nations set up various agencies which it hoped would help people in need and so bring about a better world for everyone.

- The International Court of Justice meets at The Hague in the Netherlands. Fifteen judges from different countries hear cases to do with international disputes, such as frontiers.
- The United Nations International Children's Emergency Fund looks after needy children everywhere.
- The World Health Organisation fights disease and promotes good health. In 1967 the WHO launched a campaign to wipe smallpox off the face of the earth. In 1977 a man from Somalia was the last known person to die from the disease, and two years later the whole world was smallpox free.
- The United Nations Educational, Social and Cultural Organisation promotes all aspects of learning and understanding.

Source E

Learning to read in Morocco, 1960. Part of UNESCO's work.

Things to do

1 Look at Source A.
  a Where do you think power lies in this organisation?
  b What problems might arise because of this structure?

2 Read Source B.
  This Charter sets out the aims of the United Nations. Which aim do you think would be the most difficult to fulfil? Explain why you chose this one.

3 What warning was the artist of Source C giving?

4 Look at the list of United Nations activities on this page.
  Which activity do you think would do most to help the people of the world lead better lives? Explain why you made this choice.

3.6 THE UNITED NATIONS: AN ORGANISATION FOR WAR?

One of the aims of the United Nations was to keep peace between the nations of the world. Keeping the peace, however, often meant going to war!

Korea (1950–3)

UN troops (mainly from the USA) were sent to help South Korea when it was invaded by communist armies from North Korea.

Suez (1956)

British, French and Israeli forces invaded the area around the Suez canal. The United Nations demanded their withdrawal and sent troops to keep the peace.

Arab-Israeli conflict

For ten years (1957–67) UN forces patrolled the frontier between Israel and Egypt. When they left, the Arab-Israeli war broke out.

The Congo (1960)

When the Congo became independent in 1960, law and order quickly broke down. The UN sent an army of 20,000 troops, from Canada, India, Ireland, Ghana and Nigeria, to restore peace. It also sent experts to help the country become truly self-governing and teams of doctors and food experts to help the people.

Did the UN always intervene when peace was threatened?

The UN did not intervene directly in world crises like the rebellion in Hungary (1956), the Cuban missile crisis (1962), the Vietnam War (1959–75) or the Falklands War (1982). This was either because the Security Council and General Assembly could not agree about what should be done, or because the Great Powers simply ignored them.

Source A

HISTORY DOESN'T REPEAT ITSELF

The cartoonist is saying that the only way the UN can avoid the same failure as the League of Nations is by taking military action (as in Korea). Unlike the League, the UN could use force. It had no army of its own, but members loaned troops when necessary.

Source B

Written in 1957 by the historian David Thomson.

The power of the veto was highly valued by members of the Security Council. However, the veto made the Security Council ineffective when it came to taking action against the two superpowers, the USA and the USSR.

Part of Operation 'Desert Storm'. Katherine Jenerette is on the right.

Source C

Operation Desert Storm

On 2 August 1990, Iraq invaded the tiny, oil-rich state of Kuwait in the Persian Gulf. What happened then?

- *2 August* The UN Security Council condemned the action and demanded the withdrawal of Iraqi forces.
- *9 August* The UN Security Council imposed economic and **military sanctions** on Iraq.
- *25 August* The UN Security Council called for the use of force, if necessary, to make Iraq withdraw from Kuwait.
- *29 November* The UN Security Council set a deadline of 15 January 1991 for withdrawal of Iraqi troops.
- *15 January* The deadline expired and Iraqi troops remained in Kuwait.
- *17 January* 200,000 Allied forces began 'Operation Desert Storm' with a massive air offensive to liberate Kuwait.
- *26 February* Kuwait was liberated.
- *2 March* The UN called on Iraq to revoke all claims on Kuwait.
- *5 April* The UN approved the cease-fire and called upon Iraq to respect boundaries, pay war compensation and destroy chemical, biological and nuclear weapons.

KATHERINE JENERETTE

Katherine Jenerette took part in 'Desert Storm' as a member of the US Army's 3rd Armoured Division. She was nicknamed 'Desert Kate'. This is part of what she wrote about her experiences:

Desert Storm was exciting but at the same time in the back of my mind I thought 'I could really die' so it was also very scary.

I remember taking our gas masks everywhere – the bathroom, the shower, even when I was out jogging.

*My adventures included black-out driving through the desert to find a telephone satellite site, feeding cookies to camels, dust storms, **scuds** overhead, keeping as much 5.56 ammo in my web gear as I could carry for my M-16 and, the hardest part, losing a friend killed by a land-mine.*

What were we really fighting for? Us soldiers knew we were fighting to protect America's way of life – OIL. We knew the oil in the Middle East was definitely necessary for our country and our way of life. We were not there to help spread democracy, we were there to ensure that the United States' vital interests in that part of the world were secure.

Things to do

1 Look at Source A and use the information on that page.
Would you agree that the UN has to be able to raise a fighting force if it is to be useful?

2 Read Source B and look back to the structure of the UN on page 80.
- **a** What was the veto?
- **b** Why might a country use it?
- **c** Why could using the veto mean that the UN could not carry out its job?

3 **a** Read the chronology of 'Operation Desert Storm'.
Why did the UN go to war against Iraq?
- **b** Now read about Katherine Jenerette. What does she say about why US troops were fighting Iraq?

4 Do you think countries ever act out of a real desire to make the world a better place, or are they always going to do what is in their own best interests?

3.7 POSTWAR BRITAIN: EARLY CHILDHOOD MEMORIES 1947–52

Memories are an extremely important source of information for historians. Of course, sometimes the memories are inaccurate because a person has not remembered things clearly or did not really know what was going on in the first place.

This unit and the next tell the story of Britain after the war through the eyes of a child living at this time (marked ●) and in the words of a historian (marked ◇).

Bomb-sites and re-building

● Everywhere you went in London there were bomb sites. The houses on either side would be shored up and on their outside walls, which were once inside the missing house next door, you could still see wallpaper, fireplaces, and sometimes a shelf or washbasin hanging at a crazy angle. Rosebay willow herb grew all over the ground and in the nooks and crannies of the walls.

◇ The government backed the production of thousands of pre-fabricated single-storey houses made from steel frames with asbestos panels. The first 'prefab' was put up in 1944. They were meant to last for ten years but some people were still living in them in the 1990s. The government's long-term planning was to build new towns out in the countryside.

The National Health Service

● One morning Dad went to see our doctor to ask about the new National Health Service. The doctor said: 'Mr Dawson, I didn't think you wanted that kind of service'. But we joined all the same.

◇ In 1946 the government passed a National Health Act. This provided free medical, dental and eye care treatment for everyone. It was all paid for from people's taxes. A public opinion survey in 1956 found that 96% of people wanted the new system.

The Festival of Britain

● My grandparents took me all over London when I was a child. They wanted to take me to the Festival of Britain. All my friends went. But for some reason Mum and Dad wouldn't let me go and they wouldn't take me themselves. I still don't know why. Gran and Grandpa brought me back a tartan pencil case. It didn't seem the same, somehow!

◇ The Festival of Britain was held on the south bank of the river Thames in 1951. A fun-fair and exhibition halls, a concert hall, theatre, cafés and restaurants were built and gardens laid out. The Royal Festival Hall and the gardens around it are all that is now left.

Source A

The Halls and Skylon of the Festival of Britain.

A British Restaurant.

Shopping and rationing

- I used to go shopping for my mother. This could sometimes take a whole morning even though the shops were just round the corner. Most of the time was spent queuing – especially for bread and meat. One day word went round that a certain shop had some 'viyella' material. My mother and her friends queued for hours. For years afterwards you would know whose mother was in that queue because the children had dresses and skirts, blouses, shirts and shorts all made from either pale blue or pale pink spotted viyella!
- ◇ In May 1946 a world wheat shortage led to the rationing of bread, something that hadn't happened even in the darkest days of the war. Gradually, however, wartime rationing ended: clothing, tinned foods and soap in 1949 and 1950; tea in 1952; chocolate, sweets, eggs and sugar in 1953; coke, margarine, butter, cheese, meat and bacon in 1954, and coal in 1958. Other goods were 'rationed' because they were in such short supply.

Eating out

- Every week I went with my mother to the British restaurant. It was in a long, low white building by the railway bridge. There was a counter where you queued for your lunch. We sat at wooden trestle tables and the chairs were wooden and folded flat when they weren't being used. I don't know whether or not the restaurant opened every day but we always went on a Thursday.
- ◇ British restaurants provided cheap, nutritious meals for anyone who needed them. The cost was subsidised by the government.

Fighting fathers?

- Friends laughed at me because during the war my Dad joined the Home Guard. At the start it was called the 'Local Defence Volunteers'. My Mum called it the 'Look, Dive and Vanish brigade'. My friend Gillian's father was a dispatch rider in Italy. That was terribly glamorous. When I went round to tea he cooked us marvellous spaghetti bolognese. It was quite different from the spaghetti in tomato sauce I had at home, which came out of tins.
- ◇ The Local Defence Volunteers (soon called the Home Guard) were formed in 1940 to help in the defence of Britain against German invasion. About 500,000 men were recruited and equipped with British, Canadian and American weapons. The Home Guard also manned anti-aircraft and coastal defences. It was dissolved on 31 December 1944.

3.8 POSTWAR BRITAIN:
SCHOOLGIRL MEMORIES 1952 ONWARDS

Changing schools

● *When I was in the top class in primary school I took the 11+ examination. We all did. We had been taking practice papers for weeks. This one exam decided which school you went to next. We all wanted to go to grammar school and not just any old grammar school, but the best one in our city. No one wanted to go to a secondary modern school. The results came out two days before my eleventh birthday. I was promised a bike if I passed and a tennis racquet if I didn't. But I found the bike hidden in our shed, so I knew I would get it no matter what happened!*

◇ In 1944 Parliament passed an Education Act which said that there were to be three types of secondary school: grammar, modern and technical. Children were allocated to the school which would be best for them. In 1965 the Labour government required all local education authorities to submit plans to reorganise their schools as comprehensives. In 1970 the Conservative government said education authorities could choose not to do this, but the move to comprehensives went on.

Capital punishment

● *In English lessons we often had debates. Someone would be chosen to propose the motion and someone to oppose it. They made formal speeches and then anyone could join in the argument. At the end we voted. Sometimes the debates were on silly topics, like 'This House believes cats make better pets than dogs.' But in 1955 Ruth Ellis was hanged for shooting her lover whom she had discovered was unfaithful to her. We debated the rights and wrongs of capital punishment and the arguments on both sides were passionate and angry. I made up my mind then about what I believed and I haven't changed it since.*

◇ In 1957 Parliament passed a Homicide Act which abolished hanging except for murderers who killed a police officer, or killed whilst stealing or by shooting or by explosion. In 1965 the death penalty was abolished for five years as an experiment. In 1969 Parliament made the abolition permanent.

Equal opportunities

● *When we were about sixteen, a woman came to school to tell us about the different careers that were open to girls. They ranged widely, from airline pilot to plumber. But at the end she gave herself away. 'Whatever anyone says', she declared, 'the best jobs for women are nursing and teaching.' Our teachers were furious. They had been working hard to convince us that any career was within our grasp. In one sense they were right. But they never told us of the battles we would have as women in a man's world.*

◇ In 1970 the Equal Pay Act stated that from 1975 men and women should receive equal treatment in pay and conditions where they were doing similar work, or work which evaluation tests had shown to be comparable. Discrimination through separate pay scales, or separately negotiated agreements affecting only one sex, were illegal. In 1975 Parliament set up the Equal Opportunities Commission, which investigated complaints from people who believed they had been discriminated against because of their sex.

Source A

The Aldermaston March.

Protest

- *With some friends I joined the Campaign for Nuclear Disarmament (CND). We wore campaign badges on our blazers until the school banned them. We went to local group meetings and marches. I wanted to go on the big Easter march to Aldermaston, but my parents forbade me. I was furious. In the summer, without telling them, I went to a demonstration in Trafalgar Square. It ended with a sit-down peaceful protest – and we were all taken away in police vans. Luckily I wasn't charged. In those days we believed we could change the world.*

◇ The first British hydrogen bomb was tested in May 1957. Other tests followed. In 1963 the USSR, the USA and Great Britain agreed to a test-ban treaty which stopped all testing of nuclear weapons above ground, in outer space or under water. But underground tests were still permitted and nuclear weapons were still part of the **arsenal** of all Great Powers.

Divorce and pregnancy

- *Two major events happened in my class when I was about fourteen. Mary Machie's mother divorced her father. No one spoke to her about it. It was something so shocking that no one knew what to say. No one's parents got divorced and so something unspeakably dreadful must have happened. In the same year Janet Wilson got pregnant. We listened in fascinated horror to her stories of unsuccessful secret visits to a back-street abortionist and then to rows at home when she had to tell her parents. We watched her gymslip for tell-tale signs of swelling. We wondered when the teachers would find out. One day Janet just wasn't there. We heard that she had been sent to live with an aunt until the baby was born and that her mother was going to bring the baby up as if it was hers. We never saw her again.*

◇ In 1967 Parliament passed the Abortion Act, which allowed abortions to be performed legally if there was a threat to the mental or physical health of the mother; if the child was going to be severely handicapped; or if the child was likely to be born into undesirable conditions.

In 1969 Parliament changed the law about divorce. The only ground for divorce was to be 'irretrievable breakdown' of the marriage. Proof would be separation for two years if both partners agreed; five years if not.

Things to do

Which do you think is best for finding out about postwar Britain – the memories or the historian's writing? Explain why.

Modern-day South Africa is a multi-racial society where people of different colours and races are equal in the eyes of the law. But this was not always the case. Indeed until 1994 South Africa was known throughout the world as the country where the Black majority was excluded from having a say in the running of its country by the White minority.

Early settlement

Until the mid 17th century South Africa was the home of black native Africans. From that time European settlers began to arrive in the Cape. The first settlers were Dutch, but they were soon followed the British who quickly gained control of the area. So the Dutch settlers (usually called Afrikaners) moved north and established two of their own provinces, the Transvaal and the Orange Free State. The British won control of these areas in 1902 and eight years later joined them with the two British provinces, Cape Colony and Natal to form the Union of South Africa.

White control

Although they made up only 15% of the population of the country, the Whites were in complete control of South Africa. Only Whites could be elected to Parliament and all the best jobs and land were restricted to them. In 1913 the government of the Union passed the Native Land Act which said that black Africans could not own land in 90% of South Africa. They were to be restricted to native reserves and had to carry special passes before they were allowed to enter White areas. Later laws restricted rights for black Africans at work and even forbade them from marrying Whites.

The black Africans formed their own organisation called the African National Congress (ANC) to campaign for equal rights. The ANC believed in non-violent protest, but it soon faced problems which made non-violent protest very difficult.

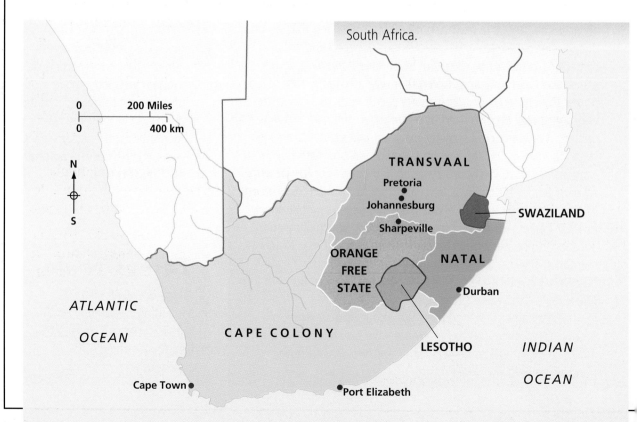

South Africa.

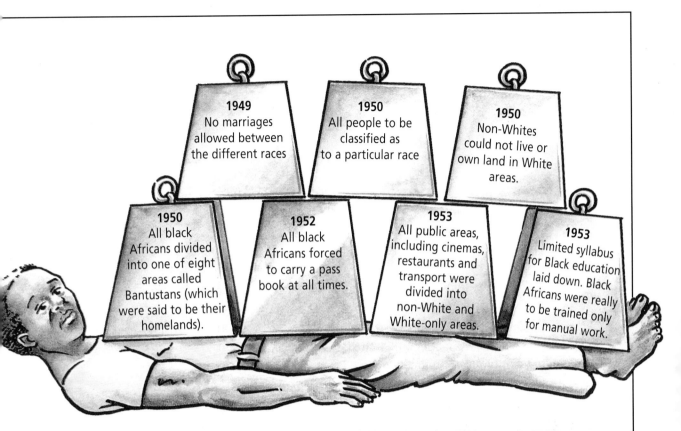

1949
No marriages allowed between the different races

1950
All people to be classified as to a particular race

1950
Non-Whites could not live or own land in White areas.

1950
All black Africans divided into one of eight areas called Bantustans (which were said to be their homelands).

1952
All black Africans forced to carry a pass book at all times.

1953
All public areas, including cinemas, restaurants and transport were divided into non-White and White-only areas.

1953
Limited syllabus for Black education laid down. Black Africans were really to be trained only for manual work.

The establishment of Apartheid 1949-53.

The establishment of Apartheid

In 1948 the Nationalist Party took office and introduced **apartheid** in South Africa. That is, it passed laws to ensure that the country was formally separated according to racial type. People in South Africa were classified according to one of four racial groups: Black, White, Asian or Coloured (mixed race). Their rights depended largely upon which group they belonged to. White supremacy was made official and the rights of non-Whites restricted by law.

Opposition to Apartheid

The non-white population of South Africa was horrified by the introduction of apartheid. In 1950 the ANC called a national strike to protest. Then in 1954 opponents of apartheid drew up the 'Freedom Charter' calling for the ending of apartheid.

In 1960 thousands of opponents of apartheid demonstrated outside a police station at Sharpeville. The police panicked and 67 black Africans were shot dead.

The incident inflamed anti-apartheid opinion and there were widespread demonstrations. The government was forced to impose a state of emergency in which almost 12,000 people were imprisoned without trial. The ANC decided to abandon its policy of non-violence and arrests soon followed, including the ANC President, Chief Albert Luthuli. Two other leading ANC members, Walter Sisulu (imprisoned 1963) and Nelson Mandela (imprisoned 1964) were to each spend 26 years in prison for opposition to apartheid.

During the same period 69 black Africans died as a result of police 'interrogation'. It was said that they had died as a result of accidents such as 'slipping and fatally injuring themselves', but everyone knew what this really meant.

Source A

An account from a journalist who witnessed events at Sharpeville in 1960.

We heard the chatter of the machine gun, then another. There were people running towards me and I kept on taking pictures as I lay on the grass. Hundreds of women rushed past us. Some of them were laughing; they must have thought that the police were firing blanks. Hundreds of kids were running too. One little boy had an old black coat, which he held up behind his back, thinking perhaps that it might save him from the bullets.

One of the policemen was standing on top of an armoured car firing his machine gun into the crowd. When the firing stopped nobody was moving in our field. They were either wounded or dead. 'Let's go before they get our film', I said.

Things to do

1 Look at the headlines in Source B. Can you explain why the South African government introduced each measure?

2 Look at Source A
The police say that they opened fire at Sharpeville because they were under threat. Does this source prove that they were not telling the truth?

3 What can you learn about South Africa at this time from Source C?

4 Read the section on Steve Biko.
If the police killed Steve Biko why do you think the inquest cleared them of any wrongdoing?

The world reaction

There was widespread opposition to apartheid from around the world, particularly in black countries. In 1960 South Africa was forced to leave the Commonwealth. In 1962 the United Nations imposed a trade **boycott** on South Africa. But many foreign countries simply found a way round the sanctions. South Africa was wealthy and they wanted to trade with it.

Pressure was also applied through sport. In 1968 the England cricket team was due to tour South Africa. It picked the South-African born mixed race player, Basil D'Oliveira in its team. The South African government said that D'Oliveira would not be welcome and so England cancelled the tour. There were no cricket matches between the two countries for another 25 years. Sport with South Africa became unacceptable to many people and other sports and other countries soon followed the English cricket authorities' lead.

Apartheid under attack

Despite international opposition apartheid continued and so did the demonstrations

Source B

Headlines in the English newspaper, *The Times*, in September 1968.

Vorster says MCC team unacceptable in South Africa

D'Oliveira 'political cricket ball'

MCC call off tour of South Africa

Feeling of disgust over ban

A cartoon published in a South African newspaper in 1959. On the sign the writing is in English and Afrikaans.

STEVE BIKO

Steve Biko was a leader of opposition to apartheid who died in police custody in 1977. Biko was one of the founders of a group called the Black Consciousness Movement in the 1960s and was arrested on several occasions before finally being taken into custody in August 1977. He was thirty years old and in good health. One month later he died of brain damage. The police claimed that he hit his head against a wall whilst being restrained. After five days, when it was realised how badly injured he was, he was driven hundreds of kilometres on the floor of a police car to hospital. He did not recover. There was a international outcry, but the official inquest acquitted the police of any wrongdoing. More recently, on 11 September 1997, a police witness admitted to the Truth Commission (see page 92) that Biko died as a result of severe beatings from the police.

against it in South Africa. There was particular resentment in the townships (poor areas of towns and cities where black people lived). In 1976 15,000 pupils in a township demonstrated against the government announcement that in future all lessons were to be in Afrikaans. They saw this not only as a foreign language but also as the language of their oppressors. Police opened fire and a number of children were killed. Once more there was an outbreak of violence and once more the government introduced tough measures.

The beginning of the end

In 1978 P.W. Botha became President. He realised that apartheid could not be maintained by force and decided to win support of those Blacks who had skilled jobs by watering down apartheid. He hoped to be able to divide opposition to apartheid. So he allowed Blacks to buy property in White areas, join unions and receive a better education. He even allowed mixed marriages and abolished the requirement to carry a pass book.

But Botha's reforms did not work. Black Africans wanted equality, not a few changes. In 1983 the United Democratic Front (UDF) was set up to campaign against apartheid and included many Whites. A leading member of the organisation was Archbishop Desmond Tutu. There was also opposition to the government from White extremists such as Eugene Terre Blanche and his Afrikaner Resistance Movement, which opposed any changes to the apartheid system.

More clashes

Although the UDF opposed violence, rioting became increasingly common and divisions within the Black community were also shown. Chief Buthelezi's Inkatha Party criticised the ANC and there were often clashes between ANC and Inkatha supporters. In places this led to horrific murder by '**necklace**'. Some areas of the country became almost ungovernable and Botha was forced to declare a state of emergency once more. Police brutality increased and international opposition to apartheid led to foreign companies withdrawing from South Africa and the tightening up of sanctions. However, Mrs Thatcher argued that sanctions merely harmed Black people and so Britain did not join in the boycott – though thousands of Britons refused to buy South African goods from supermarkets.

Apartheid ended

In 1989 President Botha resigned through ill health and was replaced by F.W. de Klerk. He realised the need to make concessions to the Blacks. He removed the ban on the ANC and finally released Nelson Mandela from prison in 1990. Mandela then called off ANC's campaign of violence against the government.

The new South African flag.

One man one vote

During 1991 and 1992 talks were held to establish a new constitution based on 'one person one vote'. Not surprisingly these talks proved very difficult and it was only after great efforts by both sides that a 'Record of Understanding' was reached. It was agreed that the first multiracial elections in South African history would take place in April 1994. Mandela and de Klerk were awarded the Nobel Peace Prize for bringing about the agreement.

The new government

The results of the 1994 election put the country in the hands of the ANC, which won 62.6% of the vote. Nelson Mandela became President and another ANC representative, Thabo Mbeki, became First Deputy President. F.W. de Klerk's National Party scored the second highest number of votes and he became Second Deputy President. Of the 27 seats in the Cabinet, ANC took 18, the National Party 6 and Inkatha 3.

The Truth Commission

In 1996 the Truth and Reconciliation Commission began its work in South Africa. Its task was to unearth the truth of the atrocities that had occurred under apartheid and so help the country 'heal its wounds'. In order to get people to testify before it the Commission granted an amnesty to those testifying, so that they would not be frightened to admit what they had done. The commission also heard accounts from the relatives of victims.

But the truth does not always help heal, especially as those testifying are exempt from criminal proceedings. In 1984 the wife and daughter of Marius Schoon were blown apart by a bomb planted by the security forces. Marius now knows that Craig Williamson, a government spy, played a part in the bombing. 'Suddenly their deaths are in the forefront of my mind again', he says. 'Now it is personal. There is a good chance that I may actually shoot Williamson'.

Nelson Mandela.

The 'Rainbow' country

It was hoped that this new government would lead the new 'rainbow' country to a period of racial harmony and prosperity. The first signs of this came when black and white South Africans stood side by side to cheer their country to victory in the rugby World Cup in 1995. But there is still much work to do and since the formation of the new government both Chief Buthelezi and F.W. de Klerk have resigned because of opposition to ANC policies.

Source E

An article from the English newspaper, the *Guardian*, 27 February 1998.

SECURITY POLICE PLOTTED MANDELA ASSASSINATION

It has been alleged that members of South Africa's now disbanded security forces hired an extremist hitman to shoot Nelson Mandela at his presidential inauguration ceremony in front of world-wide television audiences in 1994.

The extraordinary story emerged after an informer admitted to Archbishop Desmond Tutu's Truth Commission that he was hired for £31,000 to shoot Mr Mandela in an assassination which would have stunned the world and probably resulted in civil war. He pulled out after he heard that security officers planned to shoot him immediately after the assassination and then claim the credit.

Detectives investigating the claims are said to have arrested a senior police officer and seized two high powered rifles.

Things to do

1 In the 1980s the black people of South Africa wanted foreign countries to stop trading with their country. Why did Britain not do so?

2 Why do you think President de Klerk finally let Nelson Mandela out of prison?

3 Why do you think the ANC did so well in the 1994 elections?

4 Why was winning the rugby World Cup in 1995 so important to South Africa?

5 Read the section on the 'Truth Commission'.
   a What is its purpose?
   b Why has it given an amnesty to those appearing before it?
   c Why has this angered some South Africans?
   d In what ways can the work of the commission be said to be bringing further pain to some South Africans?

6 What can we learn about South Africa from Source E?

GLOSSARY

Britain 1750-1900
(pages 4–97)

abolitionists people who wanted slavery abolished, and who campaigned for this cause.

acquitted not guilty

apprentice someone who is learning a trade by working for a master for a certain period of time, for very low wages, and sometimes no wages at all, just food and lodgings.

aristocrats members of the highest class in society.

blight a plant disease caused by fungus or insects

brimstone an early word for sulphur, a yellow chemical element.

carding the action of 'combing' wool which has come straight from the fleece, to make it free from tangles so it can be spun.

chaff the husks around the grains of crops, that are separated by shaking.

Chartist someone who believed in the Chartism movement for social and electoral reform in the mid-nineteenth century.

commissions groups set up by the government to investigate issues

confirmation a religious ritual, confirming a baptised person as a member of the Christian Church.

consul a chief magistrate, appointed to head the government.

cudgels short, thick sticks, used as weapons.

depots storehouses

domestic service working as a servant in a household, for example, scullery maid or cook.

drayman someone who drives a horse and cart for a brewer.

emigrated left your country of birth to live in another country.

entrepreneur someone who gets involved in lots of businesses and enterprises, with the risk of profit or loss.

epidemic a disease that kills a lot of people in one outbreak.

evicted made to leave one's rented home, because of non-payment of rent.

excursion trains trains which were intended to take people on journeys for pleasure, not business.

floggings beatings with a whip or stick as punishment.

gauze a fine mesh of wire that lets light through.

goods produce of a country, which can be traded.

guillotine a machine with a heavy, sharp blade that drops down, used for beheading.

hayricks another word for a haystack – a packed pile of hay with a pointed top.

hearse the vehicle which carries the coffin at a funeral.

hovels small, roughly-made houses, usually with only one room, made from mud and straw, and thatched.

indenture a settled agreement or contract between an apprentice and his/her employer.

independence freedom for a country to rule itself, and not be under the authority of another country.

indigo a natural blue dye, which comes from the indigo plant

inoculation giving someone a very small dose of a disease, so they can build up immunities to that disease, preventing them from getting it again.

ironworks a factory where iron goods are made.

keep food and lodgings.

knighted awarded a title by a monarch, in return for good service.

liberty freedom

marines a body of troops trained to serve on land or sea.

martyrs people who are punished because of their beliefs.

mechanisation the introduction of machines to do factory work, instead of manual labour.

morality a set of moral 'rules' which people consider to be right and proper.

music hall an evening of music and entertainment at a theatre or hall.

penal colony a colony to which people are **transported** as a punishment from the country which owns the colony.

pitching rolling and lurching violently from one side to another.

plantations estates, usually in colonies, on which tobacco, cotton, sugar and other products are grown. Plantations were usually worked on by slaves.

planters the managers of **plantations.**

plundering robbing a place of its goods, especially in war.

reformers people who wanted reform. People who wanted things to change according to their ideals.

repealed withdrawn from government.

revolution the overthrow of a

government in favour of a new system.

scullery a small room, usually at the back of the kitchen, used for washing dishes and pots.

seed potatoes those potatoes which are grown for planting again next year, not for eating.

socialist someone who believes that the community as a whole should control production and distribution of goods.

sub-let allow somebody to rent property from you, when you are renting the property in the first place.

telephone exchange the central telephone office, where calls were taken and transferred.

transported sent to a **penal colony** instead of prison, as a punishment.

Viceroy someone who rules on behalf of a monarch if the monarch does not live in that country.

workhouses houses where people who were too poor to support themselves were sent, to work for their **keep**. Workhouses were made as uncomfortable as possible, in an attempt to make them unattractive to slackers and idle people.

Twentieth Century World
(pages 98–187)

abdicate stand down from power.

appeasement calm down an enemy by making concessions to them.

armistice a stopping of war, by a truce made by both opposing sides.

arsenal the store of weapons held by a person or government.

billeted placed with families whom the government had asked to look after the evacuees.

black market selling hard-to-get goods (especially those on ration) illegally.

blitzkrieg a sudden and heavy military attack, done to gain a quick victory.

buffer zone an area of safety.

bund a Jewish socialist organisation set up in 1897 in Vilna, Poland. It supported and organised workers, upheld cultural rights, formed self-defence squads and worked actively against anti-Semitism.

collaborate work together with.

communist someone who believes in Communism. Communism was a theory of government developed by Karl Marx. He believed that war between the classes should lead to a state where everything is publicly owned and shared out according to what people need.

consolidate make strong and stable.

convoys groups of vehicles travelling together.

democratic in favour of social equality.

dictator someone who rules alone with total authority.

fascist someone who was in favour of fascism. Fascism was a very right-wing **nationalist** movement.

guerrilla an unofficial soldier, usually a member of a political group, who takes part in sabotage and ambushes instead of conventional war.

hyper-inflation excessively high inflation in prices.

militant aggressively active, especially in relation to politics.

nationalist an extreme patriot

police state a state controlled by political police who oversee all activities.

propaganda publicity specially selected to put forward one point of view, usually political.

purser the officer in charge of the accounts on a ship.

radar a system whereby objects can be detected even when they are far away, by bouncing radio waves off them.

recession when the economy is doing badly.

reparations an amount paid out to make amends for something. Countries pay reparations after war as a punishment.

republic a state in which power is held by the people, or their elected leaders, instead of a monarch or supreme leader.

military sanctions military action imposed on one country by another, to try and make the first country conform to a set of rules or a way of government.

scapegoats people to blame for something, even though it wasn't their fault.

scuds short range missiles of mass destruction.

subversion seeking to overthrow a government or regime.

totalitarian a dictator style of government.

tribunal a board set up to judge over a matter of public concern

Heinemann Educational
Halley Court, Jordan Hill, Oxford   OX2 8EJ
a division of Reed Educational and Professional
Publishing Ltd

OXFORD CHICAGO PORTSMOUTH NH (USA)
MELBOURNE AUCKLAND IBADAN GABORONE
JOHANNESBURG

Heinemann is a registered trademark of
Reed Educational and Professional Publishing Ltd

ISBN 0 435 30963 3
99 00 01 02 5 4 3 2

British Library cataloguing in Publication data
for this title is available from the British Library

Printed in Spain by Mateu Cromo

Illustrations by Sally Artz, Stephen Wisdom and
Visual Image.

Photographic acknowledgements

The authors and publisher would like to thank the
following for permission to reproduce photographs:

Cover photograph: Bridgeman/Manchester City Art
Library, Imperial War Museum

Britain 1750-1900

AKG: 3.5D
Birmingham City Library: p5D
Bradford Libraries: 2.8A, C, 2.9A, B, C, D
Bridgeman: 1.1A, 1.2G, 2.13F, 2.14D, 3.4B, 3.5B,
British Museum: p4A
Cfarthfa Castle: 2.14A, B
Catherine Emmerson: 3.9A
e.t. Archive: 1.1C, 2.1D, 2.2A
Fotomas: 1.6B, 2.5M
Getty Images: 1.4B
Giraudon: 3.3A
Chris Honeywell: 2.5E
Hulton Getty: 1.5B
J. Meakin: 2.3D

Katz: 2.1C, 2.7A
Lancaster City Museums: 1.2D
Mary Evans: p7F, 1.6C, 1.7B, 2.5A, C, D, 2.11A,
2.12F, 2.13A,
Michael Holford: 1.4A
Museum of English Rural Life: 3.9C
National Library of Wales: 3.7B, D
National Portrait Gallery: 1.1B
National Trust: p4B
Paul Revere Memorial Association: 3.2C
PRO: 3.6D
Punch: 2.5H, 3.6C
Quarry Bank Mill: 2.10A, B, C, 2.11B, C
Salvation Army: p6E
Sotheby's: 1.2H
The Science Museum: 2.1A
Thomas Nelson: 1.3A
Topham: 2.1B
Wansdworth Library: p5C
West Sussex Record Office: 2.14C

Twentieth Century World

AKG: 2.1A, C, 2.4D
Punch/Centre for the Study of Cartoons: 2.4A
Bridgeman: 1.2B
Corbis: 2.11D
e.t. Archive: 1.3E, 2.13H
Getty: 2.5A, F
Hulton Getty: 1.4B, 2.1B, 2.3D
Imperial War Museum: 1.2C, E, 1.3C, 1.4H, 2.3B,
2.8A, C, p143, 2.11A, 2.12B, 2.14F
Katherine Jenerette: 3.6C
Katz: 3.4D
Kobal Collection: 3.3B
Liddle Collection/University of Leeds: 1.3B
David Low/Centre for the Study of Cartoons: 3.5C,
3.6A
Magnum: 2.9A
Mary Evans: 1.3A, 1.4A, C, 2.10B
Mirror Syndication: 2.10C
Museum of London: 1.4G
Nationalmuseet Denmark: 2.7B
Popperfoto: 2.10A, 2.11E, 2.14A, 3.3A
SCR: 2.7D
Topham: 2.14E
Yad Vashem: 2.14B

The publishers have made every effort to trace
copyright holders of material in this book. Any
omissions will be rectified in subsequent printings if
notice is given to the publisher.